P9-DZY-415

# LOVE HIM

## — OR —

# LEAVE HIM

### *But Don't Get Stuck with the Tab*

Hilarious Advice
— *for* —
Real Women

# LONI LOVE

*with* JEANNINE AMBER

SIMON & SCHUSTER

*New York   London   Toronto   Sydney   New Delhi*

Simon & Schuster
1230 Avenue of the Americas
New York, NY 10020

The people in this book are fictionalized. Any resemblance to real people
is purely coincidental. If at any point you are reading this book and
say to yourself, "Hey, that's me!" you might want to
rethink some of your life choices.

First Simon & Schuster hardcover edition July 2013

SIMON & SCHUSTER and colophon are
registered trademarks of Simon & Schuster, Inc.

For information about special discounts for bulk purchases,
please contact Simon & Schuster Special Sales at 1-866-506-1949
or business@simonandschuster.com.

The Simon & Schuster Speakers Bureau can bring authors to your live event.
For more information or to book an event contact
the Simon & Schuster Speakers Bureau at 1-866-248-3049
or visit our website at www.simonspeakers.com.

Designed by Ruth Lee-Mui

Manufactured in the United States of America

1   3   5   7   9   10   8   6   4   2

Library of Congress Cataloging-in-Publication Data

Love, Loni.
Love him or leave him, but don't get stuck with the tab : hilarious advice for
real women / Loni Love with Jeannine Amber. — First Simon & Schuster
hardcover edition.
pp. cm.
1. Dating (Social customs)—Humor. 2. Single women—Humor.
3. Love—Humor. I. Amber, Jeannine. II. Title.
PN6231.D3L68 2013
818'.602—dc23        2012049523

ISBN 978-1-4516-9476-5
ISBN 978-1-4516-9478-9 (ebook)

This book is dedicated to my mother, Momma Love,
for her guidance and wit, and
for always steering me in the right direction.

And to my fans: the married women, single girls,
baby mommas, and chicks on the side
(because, hey, they need advice too).

# Contents

## Making Up

## Cheating

## Friends and Family

## Getting Hitched

## Messy Messy Messes

## Acknowledgments

# LOVE HIM OR LEAVE HIM

*But Don't Get Stuck with the Tab*

# INTRODUCTION

*I first felt the thrill* of entertaining back in 1972, when I was crowned Little Miss Detroit. At the pageant, I hit the stage in patent leather shoes and a starched pink dress, but I had so many braids in my hair that my tiara slid right off my head! When I bent down to pick it up, I slipped and landed on my behind. Everyone burst out laughing. But instead of feeling embarrassed I jumped up with a huge smile on my face. I realized that day that making people laugh makes me happy. In fact, it's the very reason I left my job as an engineer to become an entertainer. Most people don't know I used to be an engineer. But I was the worst engineer in America. In fact, I'd like to extend a personal apology to anyone driving a 1992 Cutlass (that was one of the projects I worked on before leaving the field to pursue my dream of being a comic). There's only one thing I love as much as making people laugh, and it's giving advice. Ask anyone who's received one of my Love Lessons and they'll tell you I have a special gift.

I've always had a good head on my shoulders. I grew up in the Brewster-Douglass Housing Projects in Detroit during the height of the crack epidemic. The streets were filled with drug dealers and prostitutes. Coming up in such a rough environment, a girl had to be tough and street-smart to survive. I saw firsthand what happens to women who are foolish in love, or just plain foolish.

When I was a teenager, Peaches was one of my very best friends. Peaches had a smile that lit up her face, and she could do *some* hair! When we were seniors in high school, Peaches started dating a new guy from the neighborhood. Peaches would brag that her boyfriend was a "businessman." I tried to tell her the truth, that her 16-year-old boo was slinging crack. But Peaches didn't care. Living in the projects could be depressing, and her boyfriend gave her a taste of the glamorous life, buying her clothes, taking her to fancy restaurants in downtown Detroit, and driving her around in a snow white Mercedes-Benz. I didn't want any part of what Peaches's boyfriend was into, so I began to distance myself from my friend. This was a big sacrifice for me because Peaches would do my Jheri curl for free.

One night, I was doing my homework at about eleven o'clock when I heard the blast of gunfire. It was common to hear shots fired in the projects, but that night was different. This sound sent a chill through my veins. A few hours later there was a knock at my door with a neighbor bringing the news—my best friend Peaches was dead. She'd been sitting outside with her boyfriend when she was hit with a bullet that I'm sure was meant for him. For all those occasions she'd done my hair, I did hers one last time, for her funeral. She was only seventeen.

Peaches's death taught me an important life lesson: too many women make sacrifices to be with men. I've seen friends compromise their safety, dignity, money, and even happiness for the sake of a relationship. But I've seen enough. Now I've made it my personal mission to remind women that we need to put ourselves first. I learned this lesson, up close and personal, watching my single mother manage her dating life. After her divorce, my mother, Momma Love, had plenty of boyfriends, but she refused to take crap from anyone. I remember one time, one of her boyfriends, Mr. Herbert, was living with us, and Momma Love found out he'd cheated on her with Miss Bernice, the Bible study teacher. The next day his clothes and his Bible were out in the trash. Her philosophy was: no woman has to put up with second-rate treatment; someone better will always come along. "Never be a side dish," Momma Love would say. "Always be the main course." It's a lesson I took to heart.

I remember the year my friends and I were all set to graduate from high school. All the girls in my class were losing their minds worrying about who was going to take them to the prom. They were getting together in the rec center after school for powwows and conferences like, "If Jimmy doesn't ask me by end-of-day Wednesday, I'm moving on to plan B and getting with the cousin of the friend of his brother, who's not as cute but has a nicer car." There were schedules, deadlines, backup plans, and emergency ditch plans should the night not go as planned. It was totally ridiculous. I told my friends, "You need to worry about yourselves. Focus on your priorities, like how you're gonna pay for that prom dress."

I don't mean to suggest I didn't have my own share of boy trouble. Back then my boyfriend Mack was the love of my life. But I decided we weren't going to have sex because I was saving myself for marriage. (Of course, that was before I realized I would be living in a coed dorm at college.) Even though I wasn't giving it up, Mack promised me he would take me to the prom, and I believed him. Well, a few weeks before the dance, Mack hooked up with my neighbor

Tisha. Of course, I immediately dumped his cheating ass. But then I found myself with no date and a beautiful hoop dress that made me look like an extra from a production of *Gone with the Wind*. After a few days of being down in the dumps, I picked myself up and decided that me and my hoop dress would go to the prom alone. That's when the phone rang. It was Mack's best friend, Albert. He'd heard that Mack and I had broken up and was wondering if I would be his date for the prom. I can still remember the shocked look on Mack's face when his friend Albert and I walked into the dance looking like a black Rhett Butler and his date, Hattie McDaniel. It was a perfect night and the moment when I first realized my mother was right: if you refuse to accept being treated poorly, something better *will* come along. There is no need to compromise who you are just to be with a man.

Because of my attitude and my confidence, I quickly became the girl who all the other girls went to for advice. I was the one who would listen to their problems and tell them what to do when they had nowhere else to turn. "Love him or leave him," I'd always say. "But don't get stuck with the tab," meaning, respect and protect yourself so you don't end up with an STD, a broken heart, or a two-year friends-and-family data plan you can't get out of.

Twenty years later I'm still spreading that same message to my fans. People see me on television, or they come out to my comedy shows, and they feel like they know me. People approach me in airports, in ladies' rooms, and in the street, talking to me like we're old friends. Like I'm their long-lost sister. Like I'm the one with the answers to all of their problems, even though we've never met.

One time a woman came up to me after a show, introduced herself as Alison, and said, "Can I ask you something?" I thought Alison wanted me to elaborate on my why-I-hate-anal-sex joke. I get that question a lot. Instead, she was seeking advice about her relationship with her husband. The two of them hadn't been intimate for five years. "You seem like a really grounded person," she said. "I really want your opinion." Although I was only half sober, I listened, considered her problem, and gave her the best advice I could: I suggested she try to spark the flame by trying some great sex tips I'd picked up from my friend Lisa, who used to work in the "business" as a "dancer," if you know what I mean. And if that didn't work, I suggested she try a sex therapist (I knew plenty of professionals to recommend, thanks to my friendship with Dr. Drew). And if *that* didn't work, I suggested Alison think about ending the marriage because she and her husband sounded more like friends than lovers and, I pointed out, her kitty cat wasn't getting any younger. After our talk, I could see the relief on Alison's face. It was as though all she really wanted was to hear someone tell her that her needs were important. As a thank-you she bought me a shot of Hennessy, and we've been friends ever since.

I have hundreds of thousands of fans on Facebook and Twitter, and sometimes it feels as though each one of them is asking for advice. People have consulted me about their sex lives, their health, their kids, and their spouses. A few women have asked how I got to be so confident. But most of all, I get questions about relationships. *How do I meet a man? How do I know if I'm ready for marriage? When can I sleep with my ex's best friend?* I love my fans, but some of ya'll got some issues!

Well, listen to Loni: you can love him or you can leave him, but always remember that putting yourself first is the most important step in finding love. That's the foundation for all the advice I give, because it's a message so many women need to hear, over and over, like multiple orgasms.

Now, in the following chapters you'll find some of the most popular, crazy, and dumb-ass questions I've ever been asked. Plus some I made up just for fun, because while I was drinking my Hennessy one night, it occurred to me that someone *should* be asking if it's okay to date your mother's ex. For the record, I don't care how fine a man is, once he's had your momma, he's off-limits. My own mother taught me that. As soon as I started dating, Momma Love explained her loyalty hierarchy: family comes first, then friends, and then, rounding up third place, are men. I learned just how important it is to put your family first after watching two sisters duke it out during a Thanksgiving dinner fiasco. What were they fighting over? A man, of course. You can read all about the sister-on-sister throw down in chapter 9. And family love triangles aren't the only topics I address. In chapter 5, you'll find words of Loni Wisdom for the woman who thinks her boyfriend is picking fights just to have makeup sex, and in chapter 6 I give tips to the wife who is wondering if she should confess to her husband exactly how much "fun" she had on her Caribbean girlfriends' getaway.

Most of my advice comes from personal experience. There's the time I went on a double date with my friend Lisa, who talked so much she scared off our dates, or the night my wig blew off right in the middle of a romantic dinner cruise. You'll even hear plenty about my cousin Skillet. Everyone has a "cousin Skillet" in the family. He's the relative who never seems to have the kind of job that can be discussed in front of children or law enforcement. Cousin Skillet might not be everyone's idea of a great catch, but as far as I'm concerned, everybody can teach you something about love and life, even if the lesson is "Don't do what I'm doing unless you want to end up on TMZ."

So curl up with your fuzzy slippers and a cup of tea (or, if you're like me, a stiff nightcap and a Heineken chaser) and enjoy *Love Him or Leave Him, but Don't Get Stuck with the Tab.* Great love advice, hilarious stories, and plenty of laughter await! And if you still want more, I'd be happy to fix you up with my cousin Skillet.

# MEETING UP

*One of the things* I love about the single life is that you get to go on a lot of first dates. I know many women dread going out with a new guy for the first time. The nerves, the awkward conversation, the not knowing if you should order the lobster because he might be a cheap-ass and expect you to go Dutch. It's true some first dates *can* be awful. Like those times you go to a fancy restaurant and your date spends more time asking the cocktail waitress about her inner-thigh tattoo than talking to you. Or you tell him you admire the relationship he has with his mother and he says, "Great, because I've invited her to join us." But instead of facing first dates with dread, consider each and every one a great opportunity to gather information while getting a free meal. On a first date a man will tell you almost everything you need to know about what kind of person he is. You just need to stay sober enough to remember the next day.

The next time you're on a first date, look around the room. If you're in a restaurant and notice that every woman there—from the coat-check girl to the manager—is giving your date dirty looks, then consider yourself warned. He probably owes them money, a phone call, or both.

When I want to know what kind of man I'm dealing with, I look at his shoes. If he's wearing some nice hard-soled shoes, I know he's solid, dependable, and is probably the type of man to carry a condom in his wallet. If he's wearing sneakers, that's okay, as long as they're clean and have laces. I don't trust a man who wears shoes that close with Velcro. That's just lazy. Now, if he shows up for dinner wearing flip-flops, you better run for the hills. A man who wears flip-flops to dinner doesn't take anything seriously. He's the kind of man who will make fart jokes when you're trying to tell him about your horrible day at work or laugh at you if you trip and fall on your ass before he checks to see if you're okay. Trust me, even if you have a cushiony ass like mine, falling on your behind hurts. The last thing you need is your man laughing at you like he's a five-year-old at the circus. You want a man who treats you like a prize, not a clown.

The other great thing about first dates is they give you a chance to refine your First Date Look—that's the outfit and hairstyle that makes you feel most comfortable, beautiful, and confident. Even if you think your date might be a dud, it's still a great opportunity to try out a new look, get a new weave, or buy yourself a dress that exposes, er . . . I mean shows off your best assets. For example, you might not know this about me, but I have exquisite knees, so whenever I'm on a date I always wear a skirt that shows them off. When I was growing up, Momma Love always used to tell me, "Don't hide your light under a bushel." Well, the same can be said about dating: don't hide your best features under a tent dress. Got good cans? Show the girls! Well-toned arms? Wear a tube top! You're going on a date, not to Bible study.

Most important of all, on a first date, pay attention to the way the man treats you. Does he give you his undivided attention, or does he check his cell phone every ten minutes? Does he order his meal before you or patiently wait until you've asked the waiter to list all the ingredients of every dish? Does he seem interested in what you have to say, or does he constantly change the topic to sex and when he's going to get some? Even the way he walks down the street with you says a lot. A man who walks side by side with a woman sees her as his equal. A man who walks ahead expects to run the show. And a man who lags behind? Why, that's an ass man! But if you're built like Sofía Vergara, then congratulations, girl! You may just have met your Mr. Right.

> # "How many times can I call him before he thinks I'm crazy?"
>
> (Everything you need to know about first impressions, first dates, and the a-hole who never called you back.)

*Dear Loni,*

*I'm a teacher. I go to school, come home, go to bed, and start the whole thing all over again. I feel like life is passing me by. Any advice for how I can get back into the swing of things?*

*Signed,*
*Getting an "F" in Fun*

Dear Fun,

Honey, life is too short to spend it grading papers. But I understand how easy it is to get caught up with work. I'm a road comic. Every week—Thursday through Sunday—I perform at night, do press during the day, and try to catch some sleep. Then I do it all over again the next week, in a different city. It got to a point where I was on the road so much that even my good friends stopped calling. In fact, the only time my phone rang was when telemarketers called. One time it was a saleswoman trying to sell me a sex aid. I didn't need a fake penis, but the saleslady and I struck up a great conversation. I had no idea dildos came in so many different shapes, colors, and sizes! As nice as Sally the Salesperson was, when I got off the phone I realized it was time to make some changes. I needed to find time for a social life and to meet a man with a real penis.

Now when I travel to another city, I make a point of meeting a friend who lives there for lunch. And when I come home, I schedule dinner dates, brunches, and get-togethers. These small steps have really improved my quality of life. It feels good to know that when the phone rings it's a friend and not someone trying to give me a two-for-one deal on pleasure sticks.

# "I'm up for dinner, movies, or skydiving."

## LONI LOVE'S THREE-STEP PLAN FOR HAVING FUN

### Step One

Write a list of ten activities you can do alone that make you feel good (List A). Here are a few examples from my list:

- Fantasize about George Clooney
- Fantasize about Denzel Washington
- Eat chicken and waffles
- Try a new recipe
- Walk in the park sober
- Walk in the park drunk
- Cook some bacon
- Get a free makeover at the expensive makeup counter
- Study Albert Einstein's Theory of Relativity (hey, I'm a former engineer)
- Break-dance

### Step Two

Write a list of five fun activities that involve other people (List B). Here's my list:

- Going to the basketball court to watch fine-ass men play
- Roller-skating (there is nothing like a big girl on wheels)
- Going to church when the men's choir is singing

- Going to brunch with my gay friends (they have the best gossip)
- Doing the Harlem shake with the neighborhood kids

## Step Three

Each week pick two things from List A and one thing from List B and put them together for a fun-filled plan of action. Here's what I did this month:

Week One: Walked in the park sober while fantasizing about George Clooney, then went to the basketball court to watch fine-ass men play ball.

Week Two: Walked in the park drunk after eating chicken and waffles, then went roller-skating.

Week Three: Got a free makeover and ate some bacon, then did the Harlem shake with the neighborhood kids.

Week Four: Fantasized about Denzel Washington while break-dancing, then went to brunch with my gay friends and discussed the Theory of Relativity.

*Dear Loni,*

*Every day I ride the train to work and almost every day I see this same good-looking man on the platform. Recently, he's begun to say "hello." How do I send him the message that I'd like to get to know him better?*

> *Signed,*
> *Lonely on the Train*

Dear Lonely,

Let me get this straight: you're hot for a guy you see on the train every morning, but after several months you've only managed to get to "hello"? Honey, you're wasting valuable time. The first thing you need to do is strike up a conversation. The easiest way to do this is by observing *your* man for clues about things he might like to discuss. (Notice how I've already claimed him as yours!) For instance, if he's reading the sports section, ask him what he thought of the game last night. Even if you don't know much about sports, just smile and nod like you understand everything he's saying. But whatever you do, don't comment if you don't know what you're talking about. I once heard a desperate girl at a sports bar say to a dude, "I can't wait to see Venus Williams play her sister at the Super Bowl this year!"

It's also a good idea to ask a guy a question he might not

have heard before. Don't be afraid to get creative. Ask him if he believes in Bigfoot or if he's ever made his own granola or how long he can hold his breath. The point is to get the man talking. Sometimes when I meet a guy I'll look him straight in the eye and ask, "So, where do you think I need plastic surgery?"

The last time I did this the guy looked thrilled. "Excellent question!" he said. Then he told me I should consider a nose job, liposuction, and a chin implant . . . for starters. I cussed him out and he explained it wasn't personal; he's a plastic surgeon. After he finished sharing his professional opinion, he handed me a flyer for a two-for-one buffet at the restaurant near his office and asked me if I'd like to go out sometime. I turned him down and slid the coupon in my purse. It just goes to show you, ask a man a good question and sooner or later you're gonna get a free meal.

# "Is that a pork sausage in your pocket?"

## LONI LOVE'S CONVERSATION STARTERS

- Are those your real teeth?
- What do I have to do to get you to change my oil...and oil me down?
- Do you think I need a bra with this dress?
- Is there any good porn for old people? I want to surprise my grandma.
- I usually drink my wine out of plastic cups. Do you think I should switch to paper for the environment?
- How many strawberry wine coolers until you're drunk enough for me to take advantage of you?
- Do you think I can fit this entire banana in my mouth?

*Dear Loni,*

*I went out to dinner with a man who left a five-dollar tip on a seventy-dollar bill. I've never gone out with a bad tipper before. What do you think this means?*

*Signed,*
*Stunned*

Dear Stunned,

This means your date's a cheap-ass. As far as I'm concerned, this is a clear signal that this man is not good boyfriend material. And I'm speaking from experience.

I once dated a cheap-ass. On our first date, he stiffed the waitress. I thought it was a mistake, but soon enough his cheap-ass-ness had him treating me like his personal Walmart. He would drop by just to "borrow" my household supplies. He'd take a little Tupperware container and fill it with laundry detergent. Then he'd pull off half a roll of paper towels. Then he'd take a kitchen knife and slice himself a piece of my soap. I tried to ignore it, but it only got worse. One day I caught him backing up his car and loading the trunk with boxes of laundry detergent and my economy packs of toilet paper. Then he went into my garage, took the garden hose, and siphoned gas right out of my gas tank . . . while I was still in my car! Looking back, I think he only dated me so he could shop at my house.

The bottom line is, don't date a cheap-ass if you're looking for love. As Momma Love always says, a man who doesn't tip well doesn't appreciate other people's hard work. That kind of man sure won't appreciate you.

# "He's a perfect boyfriend . . . if your name is Chad."

## LONI LOVE'S GUIDE TO YOUR MAN'S TRUE NATURE

| If he . . . | Then he . . . |
| --- | --- |
| yells at his mother | is a jerk |
| yells at his baby's momma | is a broke jerk |
| opens the door and walks in before you | will not satisfy you in bed, and won't even notice there's a problem |
| is rude to the waiter | has a small penis |
| calls you "dude" | is too young for you |
| is constantly buying you lingerie | wears it when you're not at home |
| always asks what you're wearing so he can coordinate his outfit to yours | wishes he were your gay best friend |
| yells at the dry cleaner | only owns one suit |
| is rude to his child's teacher | may not be able to read |
| forgets your birthday | considers you a side piece. I don't know about you, but the only sides I like are beans and rice. I'm a main course, baby! You should be too. |

*Dear Loni,*

*I reconnected with an old elementary-school friend on Facebook and we've begun dating. He seems to have led a pretty normal life in the twenty years since we last saw each other. I, on the other hand, ran away from home at fifteen and did a lot of crazy things of which I'm sure my new man wouldn't approve. How do I tell him about my checkered past without scaring him off?*

*Signed,*
*Wild Child*

Dear Wild Child,

This reminds me of the time I went on a blind double date with my friend Lisa. Lisa is a former exotic dancer who is now a successful lawyer (with no student loans to pay off, I might add, thanks to her skills on the pole). The evening started with cocktails. But after Lisa told a story that ended with her exclaiming, "And now the doctor says I'm totally not contagious!" Lisa's date excused himself to use the restroom. Shortly after, his friend, with whom I had made elaborate imaginary plans for later that evening, received an "emergency" phone call that he had to take outside. Neither of them ever came back to the table. They also left us with the bill, which really pissed me off. I wouldn't have ordered a third shot of Patrón if I knew I had to pay for it.

It's always difficult to know how a man is going to respond to your past. You don't go into detail, but I'm guessing your younger days included at least one relationship with a guy with a tattoo on his face. Can you really blame your man for being concerned? He'd probably think, *A tattoo on his face? I thought I was a badass getting this dolphin tattoo on my lower back. It really hurt.* The good news is some men are so confident, they don't care what you did before you met them. They might even joke about it, like, "Hey, babe, isn't that the guy from your sex tape?"

Right now, we don't know what kind of man you're dealing with. The easiest way to find out is to casually mention something from your past and see how he reacts. For instance, you might be out at dinner and hear some music in the background. "I like this song," you might say. "It reminds me of the time I went to a swingers party." Then look down at your menu. "The salmon looks good!" Now the ball is in his court. Does he lean forward with wide eyes and a smile and say, "I hope you used protection!" or does he start quoting Bible verses? Everything you need to know about this man will be revealed by his response. If he doesn't freak out, you can serve up a little more information, like about the stint you did in a maximum-security prison. The key is to not reveal too much too soon.

And if this guy can't get past your past, then cut him loose and, as Lionel Richie sings, "Sail on." He won't change his opinion of you and you'll make yourself crazy trying to get him to accept you.

*Dear Loni,*

*I met this guy who still spends a lot of time with his ex. He says she's one of his "best friends." My girlfriend says this is a huge red flag and that he's probably still in love. What do you think?*

*Signed,*
*[Ex]tremely worried*

Dear Worried,

This reminds me of my Uncle Jimmy, who married his high school sweetheart. Then they broke up. Then they remarried. Then they broke up again. Then last year they got married again. I told Uncle Jimmy, "I love you, but I am not buying another wedding gift!" You're probably thinking, *What does this have to do with me?* Well, in between those three marriages Uncle Jimmy and his ex were "just friends." At least that's what Uncle Jimmy told all the women he was dating. My point is, some exes are really exes, and some exes are simply "taking a break." The only way to know for sure if your man still has feelings for his ex is to observe his behavior.

Momma Love always used to say there is no man on the face of the earth able to hide his feelings when he's really in love. Remember when Tom Cruise fell in love with Katie Holmes? He jumped all over Oprah's yellow sofa, while Oprah looked on in shock. She was probably thinking, *Why is this boy putting his dirty shoes all over my furniture?* Of course, a man's not always going to jump up and down to let you know he's still in love with his ex. But that doesn't mean there won't be signs; you just need to know what to look for.

# "If it's really over, why are her panties in your underwear drawer?"

## LONI LOVE'S SIGNS HE'S NOT OVER HIS EX

- He says he "recently" got out of his past relationship, but it's been five years.
- He keeps her baby picture as the background image on his cell phone.
- She calls, and he acts like it's coming from the Oval Office and takes the phone into the other room.
- He does her yard work for free but makes you pay a gardener.
- They have a "complicated" custody agreement for their dog.
- He calls you by her name and doesn't realize it.
- His mother calls you by her name and doesn't realize it.
- He gets moody after he reads her Facebook status. Then you hear him in the next room muttering, "How come she never asked *me* to go to Six Flags?"
- He sits you down and tells you, "I am not over my ex."

*Dear Loni,*

*I have fallen madly in love with my boss. I know nothing can happen, he's happily married and I totally respect that. But how do I stop obsessing over a man I can never be with?*

> *Signed,*
> *Obsessed with the Best*

Dear Obsessed,

Girl, I know how you feel. I feel this way about my boo Dr. Drew. I met Dr. Drew years ago when I did his radio show. He pronounced a big medical word for me and I was hooked. Plus, he gives me free medical advice and a lollipop any time I want.

It's hard to stop thinking about someone you've decided is possibly your soul mate. Just like you, there were times when all I could do was think about Dr. Drew. It was especially bad on days when I was suffering with a medical emergency, like a splinter or a case of indigestion. But face it: your boss (like happily married Dr. Drew) is off-limits. He will never be with you. And if he did leave his wife to be with you, he wouldn't be the perfect person you think he is. He would be a cheater and you would be a home wrecker. And I think we know how that story turns out: before you know it, the two of you will be just like Brangelina, adopting babies from all around the world to get people to like you.

You need to break yourself out of this fantasy. Take a piece of paper and write, "My boss is married. He is off-limits." On a separate piece of paper list the things that make you and your crush incompatible. For instance, Dr. Drew specializes in helping people with addictions. Now, I'm not an addict, but I do like to take the edge off. I'm pretty sure Dr. Drew would not approve of my drinking a fifth of Hennessy with LeRoy and the gang like I do every weekend. This is what you call "lifestyle incompatible." For me, that's a deal breaker.

Now take your two pieces of paper, attach them to your bathroom mirror, and read them out loud every day before you go to work. You need your brain to recategorize this man from "potential love interest" to "someone else's husband who is *not* my soul mate and whose wife knows Brazilian jujitsu and might kill me in my sleep."

But this situation isn't all bad. In fact, it's a perfect opportunity for you to identify what you're looking for in a partner. Make a list of ten things you admire about your boss. The list might start out something like this:

**I love my boss's:**
- Integrity
- Ambition
- Family values
- Silver hair
- Good clean smell

At the bottom of the page write in big block letters, "Must be single and ready to mingle!" Now you have a master list of what you want in a man.

Looking for a man without a master list is like going to the supermarket without a grocery list. You risk coming home with a shopping cart full of Ho Hos and Ding Dongs. Let your master list be your guide. Let's say you meet a man who dazzles you with his great smile and muscles. Look at your list. Right there it says, "Must be a vegetarian." What does this good-looking guy do? He smokes his own meat in his backyard. You may think, *We can make it work*, or *Opposites attract*, or *I'll get him to change*. Girl, please! Stick to your master list. The list never lies.

# "Must cook bacon."

## LONI LOVE'S MASTER LIST

- Tall
- Knows how to give a compliment
- Loans me money but knows he won't get it back
- Does not exceed a maximum of one (1) baby momma
- Does not drink Hennessy (so there's more for me)
- Knows how to clear my pipes
- Doesn't mind sitting in the middle seat on an airplane, while I sleep on him
- Can find the United States on a map

*Dear Loni,*

*I went to lunch with a guy I met online, and had a really awesome time. After our date I sent him a text saying "thanks." He didn't reply, so the next day I called and left a message. I left another message at his office. Then I sent him another text asking if he was okay because he's not returning my calls. I was planning to go by his work to check up on him. My friend says I am being a stalker. What do you think?*

*Signed,*
*I Want a Callback*

Dear Callback,

Woman, pull yourself together! He has your number, he sees the texts, he's heard the messages. He is choosing not to respond. I know because I react the same way when I get calls and texts from my friends who are asking for money. While the first date was good for you, Awesome Date obviously has something else going on in his life. It may be his job, his kids, his parents, another girl (or a guy) . . . who knows?

I once met a man at a club. He took my number but didn't call me for seven weeks. When I asked him what took him so long, he said, "I got a new TV. I've been busy watching it." Men have all kinds of stupid reasons for not calling back. All you need to know is that whatever is going on with Awesome

Date, it is more important than getting back to you. You need to move on. You can't be putting more energy into the relationship than he is.

The upside is, you're a girl who doesn't give up. Why don't you try directing your energy toward something more productive than getting a return phone call from an idiot who doesn't know your worth? There are charities, community events, and male strip clubs that need your time. You've been focusing on a man who won't call you back, and meanwhile a stripper named Chocolate Thunder is waiting on you!

*Dear Loni,*

*I went on a blind date with this very handsome doctor and drank way too much. I'm totally mortified. But I do like this guy. Do you think I can call him again?*

*Signed,*
*Over the Limit*

Dear Over,

Well, well, well, you became Lushy Lucy on the first date. Have no fear, I know just what to do. Your question is really a variation of a question I've heard a million times before: "How do I reclaim my dignity after I've embarrassed myself?" I guess people think I am an expert in embarrassment. As a matter of fact, they're right.

Let me tell you about this one time a date took me on a very romantic dinner cruise. We were sitting on the deck of the ship, staring into each other's eyes. The sun was setting and there was a gentle breeze. Suddenly, the wind kicked up. Before I knew what was happening, a giant gust blew my wig right off! If I had remembered to put in a few extra hairpins before leaving the house I would have avoided the wig-in-the-wind incident. Instead, I was caught out there with a tiny Afro, looking like Florida Evans from *Good Times*. My date stared at me in horror. But I remained calm. I simply undid the scarf I had tied around my neck, tied it over my 'fro like a black Grace Kelly, and kept eating. Hell, it was a free dinner. I wasn't about to stop just because my hair blew away.

If you want to get over your embarrassment, you have to do exactly as I did. Act like it's no big deal. You got drunk; so what? Simply text Mr. Handsome Doctor, "I guess I overdid it with the drinking. Thank you so much for being such a gentleman." Was he a gentleman or did he take the opportunity to give you a breast exam? Who knows? You sure don't. But it doesn't matter. The point is, after an embarrassment you're responsible for setting the tone. Act like Drunk Night wasn't a big deal, and it will blow over. Just like my wig.

## "Let's talk about naked celebrities."

### LONI LOVE'S DOS AND DON'TS FOR A PERFECT FIRST DATE

- Don't get high before you go out: if it turns out to be a good date, you want to remember it.

- Don't drink too much: if you know you're a lightweight, keep it to two drinks, max. Heavyweight girls like me can handle our booze. But I still like to limit myself to four triple shots of Wild Turkey, or the moment I start slurring my words, whichever comes first.

- Don't treat the date like a job interview: unless you're in the FBI or Secret Service, you don't need to be asking your date a whole bunch of questions about his past. That's what Google is for.

- Do keep the conversation light: on a first date it's a good idea to stick to topics like sports, music, and celebrity sex tapes. "Which one is *your* favorite?" always breaks the ice.

- Do offer to pay for half the check: but if he accepts your offer, dump him. He's a cheap-ass.

# 2

# HOOKING UP

One of the best things about being in a long-term relationship is you can get plenty of lovin' with your soul mate. And one of the best things about being single is you can get plenty of lovin' with a *bunch* of people. Either way, sex is available if you want it. The problem is most women don't prepare properly before they get busy. Not preparing for sex is like not planning the seating for Thanksgiving dinner: it can be awkward, messy, and end in tears.

Before I get it on—whether with a long-term lover or a one-night stand I met on ChristianMingle.com—I always take time to get my head in the game. First, I watch a romantic movie. I like oldies but goodies. One of my favorites is *Mahogany,* starring Diana Ross and the fine Billy Dee Williams, but you can choose whatever suits your taste. Maybe you get hot and bothered watching Leo in *Titanic,* or maybe your tastes run more toward something starring Justin Bieber. Girl, I'm not gonna judge. Just keep in mind, if the sex with your partner isn't good, you may find yourself fantasizing about the lead in the movie, so stay away from anything featuring a dog or a zombie.

Once I'm in the mood, I like to give myself a pre-sex pep talk by telling myself, "You is kind, you is smart, you is important." I say it just like Viola Davis did when she played Aibileen in *The Help*. I also like to let the man know what he's in for, or as I like to think of it, give him my list of demands. I might send him a flirty text or whisper something sensual to him over dinner, such as "I got Viagra if you need it."

Of course, if you expect your man to rise to the occasion, you need to do your part to make sex enjoyable for him, and that means making sure you're in peak sex condition. I like to luxuriate in a nice warm bath, rub baby oil all over, and dab on my favorite discount designer perfume. Now, I know what you're saying: "But Loni, what if I'm having sex in the car, or the back of a club, or the coat closet of my child's classroom after parent-teacher night? How am I supposed to have a luxurious bath then?" That is a good point.

Sometimes the magic happens when we least expect it. That's why every sexually active woman should have on her, at all times, a Quickie Kit. That's where you keep everything you need for the unexpected sexual encounter. In my kit I have some condoms, some mouthwash, baby wipes, and a pair of dark sunglasses. The shades come in handy when you've been with a man in a dimly lit club and realize on your way out to the car that he's not as handsome as you originally thought. Hide your face, girl!

Other times, the best sex happens in the comfort of your own home or, if you travel a lot like I do, in the comfort of a Comfort Inn. Either way, it's important to get your environment sex-ready. That means low light, soft music, and a well-stocked bar with plenty of adult beverages. Put fresh sheets on the bed and sprinkle something nice smelling around the pillows. Depending on my date, I'll either go with lavender water or bacon bits. And don't ignore other rooms in the house. Scatter some unbreakable items, like plastic cups and old magazines, on the dining room table so when your man sweeps them onto the floor, ready to ravish you like in a Hollywood love scene, you won't be distracted thinking, *Did this idiot just break my crystal salad bowl?*

But most important, make sure you're safe. A smart woman should always have plenty of condoms. A little Love Lesson: make sure to have condoms in different sizes, because not all men are hung alike. But the thing men *do* have in common is a fragile ego. So what I do is take all the condoms, no matter how big, and put them in a box marked "Jumbo Extra-Large King Size." As any woman experienced in the ways of love knows, the best preparation for a night of good sex is letting your man think he's king.

> ## "How can I make him stay until breakfast?"
>
> (Everything you need to know about casual sex, kinky sex, and sex with your ex's brother. Because, hey, stuff happens.)

*Dear Loni,*

*I met a guy at a bar and we hooked up. He's so cute and funny, I think he might be boyfriend material. My best friend says it's impossible to turn a one-night stand into a relationship. Is she right?*

*Signed,*
*Girlfriend Material*

Dear Girlfriend,

Tell your best friend to stop hating. Women end up having sex with men they barely know for all kinds of reasons: they're horny or had too many cocktails, the sun is up, the moon is out, they're horny, they ate oysters, he smelled like an ex, or . . . they're horny. Some women are just carefree, or as men call them, "sluts." Still, one-night stands can create some awkward situations. It's uncomfortable asking a man his name after you've just re-created a scene from the porn classic *Too Many Holes and Not Enough Time*. If you want a relationship, it's much easier if you find out whether you like each other *before* you get naked. But that doesn't mean turning porn sex into a meaningful romance is impossible. I know, because I've done it myself with a guy I call Church Charlie.

I met Charlie at church; that's how he got the name. I noticed him right away because he put five hundred dollars in the offering plate. I was impressed, so I sat next to him and helped him find the scripture for the sermon. (Who knew those years of Bible study would help me meet a man?) After church, I told him I was cooking Sunday dinner and invited him over. Charlie stayed for dinner and dessert. We had a nightcap and then . . . breakfast. In the morning, instead of getting all lovey-dovey and hugging up on him, I played it cool. I pulled on my PJs, headed to the kitchen, and asked him, "You want some pancakes?" I was nonchalant and he was intrigued. Plus, I've never met a man who didn't like sex and pancakes. Charlie called me the next day, and sure enough we started dating.

The secret of turning a one-night stand into a relationship is you have to play it cool. Was I really feeling calm and collected the morning I woke up with Charlie? Of course not. I was excited I just got some, and nervous that Charlie was going to open the drawer on my nightstand and find my well-worn copy of *Fifty Shades of Grey*. That's why I snuck some Wild Turkey into my morning coffee to calm my nerves. But Church Charlie didn't need to know all that.

Of course, turning a one-night stand into a relationship can only happen if the man is open to *having* a relationship. If he wakes up and makes a run for the door before you can say, "Would you like some Wild Turkey in your coffee?" write him off. Pull out your copy of *Fifty Shades* and keep hope alive.

# "No, you can't give your parole officer my phone number."

## LONI LOVE'S SIGNS YOUR ONE-NIGHT STAND HAS NO FUTURE

- He leaves money on your bedside table.
- He asks if he can use your phone to call his sex-addiction counselor.
- He calls his mother bragging about the sex you just had.
- He takes out a little black book and crosses your name off a list.
- He calls his wife and asks her to come pick him up.
- He wakes up, looks at you and says, "Please tell me we didn't just have sex."
- As he's leaving, he asks if he can borrow some clean panties.

*Dear Loni,*

*I'm a new mother and I haven't felt like having sex since the baby. I can tell my husband is getting impatient, but I just don't feel like being touched. What should I do?*

*Signed,*
*Closed for Business*

Dear Closed,

This reminds me of when my friend Rosa had her triplets. We were in the labor room with babies coming out of her like she was a clown car. After forty-six hours of labor, she swore off sex . . . and demanded a divorce.

Of course, not everyone wants to end their marriage after giving birth, but it's perfectly normal to be turned off of sex, at least for a while. Not only did you just push a human being out of your vajayjay, you now have a tiny baby sucking on your milk makers every two hours. The last thing you want is your horny husband shoving the baby out of the way so he can get a turn.

But remember your husband has needs, too. If you're not up to lovemaking, you need to work a plan to calm your man down. Try giving him a massage complete with a happy ending. Better yet, surprise him with a BJ while he's watching the game. I recommend doing this at home, but his favorite sports bar can also work. For a nice touch, put a bowl of salsa on your back so he can keep on eating his nachos. Nothing says "I love you" like oral sex and nachos.

> ## "Not tonight, honey. And before you ask, not tomorrow night either."

### LONI LOVE'S WAYS TO SHOW YOUR MAN YOU LOVE HIM WITHOUT HAVING SEX

- Rent *Scarface, Rocky,* and the *Godfather* trilogy and curl up with him for movie night.
- Leave a jar of Vaseline on his side of the bed with a couple of naked pictures of yourself.
- Take him to an outdoor café and let him look at women's asses without your getting mad.
- Flash him a boob every now and then. Especially when he's driving.
- Challenge him to a game of *Call of Duty* and then let him win . . . and gloat about it.
- Give him a bath and finish it off with an old-fashioned hand job.
- Point to your vagina and say, "Soon!"

*Dear Loni,*

*I'm not looking for a relationship right now. How do I let a man know I'm interested in no-strings-attached sex?*

> *Signed,*
> *Hot in the Pants*

Dear Hot,

You know what kills me? The way men think that every woman they meet is looking for a relationship, as though they are all Prince Charming and we women are just damsels in distress waiting to be saved. Hell no! Men don't realize that sometimes women are busy with other things, like our careers, and we don't have time for a serious relationship. And even if we have the time, some of us just don't want to be locked down. I can relate to this 100 percent. But being single doesn't mean you have to be celibate.

The key to getting no-strings sex—and a good all-around Rule of Love—is to be clear about what you want and don't send any mixed messages. This means no doing things folks in relationships do. Don't call him "honey" or "sweetie." Don't help him strategize about his new business venture or volunteer to be his date at his best friend's wedding. Don't let him meet your momma and don't clean his apartment. And whatever you do, don't ask him questions about his *feelings*.

A man who confides in you is like a dollar store half-off sticker: stuck for good. And if you're so unlucky that he gets emotional and breaks down in front of you, you can bet he'll be showing up at your place the next day with a moving van full of his stuff, talking about how you're his "soul mate."

The bottom line is, don't get personal with a casual-sex partner. All you need to know is what size condom he wears.

# "Don't tell me about your day, just take off your clothes."

## LONI LOVE'S WAYS TO LET A MAN KNOW YOU'RE ONLY INTERESTED IN SEX

- Don't ask him his last name ... or his first.
- Tell him to make it quick because you have a real date later.
- After sex, tell him, "You don't have to go home, but you got to get the hell outta here."
- After sex make yourself pancakes and tell him he can take his ass to the nearest Denny's.
- Don't allow him to sit on any furniture, except your bed.
- Place a two-hour countdown clock by your bed; when it buzzes, throw his clothes outside.

*Dear Loni,*

*I date men, but lately I've been having sexual fantasies about my best friend, who happens to be a woman. What does this mean?*

*Signed,*
*Bi-confused*

Dear Confused,

There are only two possible explanations for your mental sexcapades:

1) You are bisexual.
2) You didn't do enough experimenting in college.

Whatever the case, you need to proceed with caution. If you put too much pressure on your friend, you might destroy the friendship. I know, because it happened to me.

Let me tell you about Stalker Susan. I met her on the comedy circuit when we were both young comics doing open-mic nights and trying to make names for ourselves. We quickly became close friends: shopping, hanging out, calling each other to gossip about which comics we thought had big penises. For about a year, everything was cool. Then one night after a show, Susan suggested we go back to my house and watch a movie. As soon as we got to my place, she complained it was too bright and started dimming the lights. Then she gave me a big hug and whispered in my ear that she thought she was falling in love with me. I turned the lights back up and told her I was flattered, but I'm straight. I said, "If I did like chicks, you'd be top of the list, girl! But I don't. So what should we watch on Netflix?"

I thought that was the end of it, but soon after I started getting text messages from her saying, "I love you," and "Let's move in together." Again I told her I wasn't interested, but she wouldn't take no for an answer. The next thing I knew, I was being stalked by my best friend. I had to end the friendship, get a new phone number, and find someone else to help me take out my weave.

Trust me, you don't want to scare off your friend the way Susan did with me. You can both end up hurt and with bad hair.

I suggest you approach the topic in a general way. Ask your friend if she's ever had a girl crush. If she shows any interest, tell her how you feel. On the other hand, if she responds to the idea of girl-on-girl love by digging into the back of her closet and pulling out her "Strictly Dickly!" T-shirt from the nineties, then it's time for you to find someone else to explore your lesbian fantasies with.

> ## "How about a game of softball, then I give you a massage?"

### LONI LOVE'S SIGNS YOUR GIRLFRIEND HAS A CRUSH ON YOU

- You invite her over for dinner and she shows up with a dozen roses and a vibrator.
- You tell her you're dating a guy and she breaks down in tears, singing Whitney's "I Will Always Love You."
- You accidentally graze her hand at the movie theater, and she starts licking your neck.
- You ask her what she wants for her birthday and she replies, "Besides you?"
- You say you need a massage and she comes over with a gallon of oil, wearing a strap-on.

*Dear Loni,*

*I've been dating this man who is super respectful and polite,
which I like. But sometimes when we're having sex, I want him
to give me a slap on the ass. How can I tell my man what I like?*

*Signed,*
*Spanky*

Dear Spanky,

I'm a firm believer that folks should talk about what they like
in bed *when they are not in bed.* Things can go very wrong when
you spring your sexual preferences on someone in the heat of
passion.

One time I was dating a pilot named Max. Max was a
great guy, very smart, and he let me fly free on his buddy
passes. One night we were getting it on and he looked at me
and said, "Call me 'Master.'" The problem was Max is the
whitest white man I've ever dated. He looks like one of the
white men you see on the TV show *Mad Men:* hair parted on
the side, crisp gray suit, and an ass so tight he walks like a
robot. I thought, *he wants me to call him Master—then what? Is
he going to start calling me Harriet Tubman? Is he going to ask me
to tap-dance? Is he going to cut some eye holes in my white bedsheets
and start wearing them around the house?*

I immediately became a civil rights activist in the bed. The action stopped and the speeches began. My point is, it's rarely a good idea to surprise a person with your unconventional sex requests while you're doing it. I suggest you tell your man you like to be spanked over a romantic dinner. That way, if he's into spanking, the dinner becomes part of the foreplay. And if he isn't into it, you still get a free dinner.

# "Yes, yes, yes . . . !"

## LONI LOVE'S GUIDE TO GETTING WHAT YOU WANT IN BED

| If you like . . . | Then . . . |
| --- | --- |
| to be choked | date a wrestler; they know when to stop |
| to be blindfolded | date a magician |
| to be handcuffed | date a cop |
| to be spanked | date a parent |
| to be with two men at the same time | date twin brothers |

*Dear Loni,*

*How long before I can sleep with my ex's brother?*

*Signed,*
*On to the Next*

Dear Next,

Girl, what did that man do to piss you off? I know it had to be something, because I've seen this behavior before.

My friend Liz once logged on to her boyfriend's Facebook account and saw a message from a chick named Samantha asking her boyfriend when they were going to get together because "it's been *soooooo* long!" Liz flipped out. She was sure her boyfriend was cheating on her and decided to get revenge by sleeping with her boyfriend's brother, Daryl. I told her I thought this was a terrible idea. But that was mostly because I wanted to sleep with Daryl myself.

The morning after Liz and Daryl hooked up, Daryl mentioned that his cousin Samantha was visiting from out of town. It turns out this was the woman Liz had seen on her boyfriend's Facebook. Liz immediately realized she'd made a huge mistake. She ruined two relationships: hers and the relationship I was planning to have with Daryl.

But maybe your intentions are more honorable. Maybe you and your ex's brother have been checking each other out for years and think being together is your true destiny. In that case, the two of you need to take your ex to a public place and tell him the truth. If you're lucky, the fear of getting arrested will stop him from punching his brother in the face. Most likely he'll just end up hating both of you. Especially you. So before you move forward with the sibling switcheroo, you need to ask yourself, "Is this worth having my ex update his Facebook status every day for the next year by calling me a ho?" Because I can tell you right now that's what's going to happen.

*Dear Loni,*

*I went on vacation and had a fling with a man I met on the beach. I don't even know his last name. I say this doesn't count. My girlfriend says it does. What do you think?*

*Signed,*
*Still a Good Girl*

Dear Good Girl,

Honestly, I don't know why some women feel that if the sex is extra slutty then they need to act like it didn't happen at all. Stop lying to yourself. You had sex. So what?

My friend Chelsea has had so many sex partners that even if she wears a snow-white dress to the church on her wedding day, by the time she gets to the altar it will look like Darth Vader is gliding down the aisle. But at least she doesn't pretend the sex never happened.

As Momma Love likes to say, all sex counts, even if it happens in the mailroom at your office with the guy who pushes the coffee cart. Anyway, you should consider yourself lucky for getting some on vacation. There are a lot of women who will never have sex on the beach, unless they order it at the bar.

*Dear Loni,*

*My boyfriend wants to know how many men I've been with before him. I've been with a lot of men. Should I tell him the truth?*

> *Signed,*
> *Been Around the Block*

Dear Been Around,

I have two words for you: hell no.

My friend Linda had a wild past. When Linda got horny and she didn't have a boyfriend, she would just go online and find a random dude to hook up with. I kind of admired how she took charge of her sexuality and her passions. Then Linda fell in love. She was very committed to her boyfriend and thought they were going to be together forever. After six months of serious dating, it came time for The Big Relationship Talk. Linda's boyfriend asked how many men she'd been with before him, and she told the truth. I don't know what the number was, but it was big enough for her boyfriend to take her off his friends-and-family plan.

Honey, your past is your past; keep it that way. There is no reason this man needs to know all the details. What do you think he's going to do with the information, anyway? I'll tell you what: he's going to imagine that every man you ever introduce him to is one of the 582,899,677 you slept with in college. He's going to feel bad, you're going to feel bad, and for what? There's no upside.

I'm not a big proponent of lying, but in this case I think a little fib is the best way to end the conversation and move on to more important matters, like where he's taking you for dinner. Next time your boyfriend asks how many men there were before him, just give him a nice low number. A good rule of thumb is to take your real number, divide by seven, and subtract five.

# "I said, 'I want a divorce!' not 'I want to give you a blow job.'"

## LONI LOVE'S GUIDE TO MEN'S FAULTY HEARING

| What women say | What men hear |
| --- | --- |
| "I've only been with three men before you." | "I have slept with all your friends." |
| "I don't want a relationship." | "I want a relationship." |
| "I want a child." | "I want child support." |
| "I think I'm pregnant." | "I want to trap you." |
| "I want to break up." | "I want to get married." |
| "I'm not in love with you anymore." | "You have permission to sleep with my best friend." |

*Dear Loni,*

*I am in a serious relationship. How long before we can do it without a condom?*

> *Signed,*
> *Not a Fan of Latex*

Dear Not a Fan,

Momma Love always used to tell me that not using a condom is the biggest mistake a single woman can make. Traveling the country performing with male comics, I'm constantly reminded of just how right she is.

Every night after the shows, there are always plenty of girls who hang back to flirt with the guys. In the morning, the hotel lobby looks like a runway for the Walk of Shame: one girl after another stumbling outside, carrying her shoes in her hand and trying to remember where she left her panties. I'm sure the girlfriends of these comics are back at home thinking, *We're in love, so we don't need a condom between us.* Meanwhile the man is thinking, *My girlfriend's a cool chick . . . and so are the other five women I'm banging on the road.*

I don't advise sex without a condom unless you're married and monogamous. And even then, I'm not so sure about ditching the protection, especially if your husband is an athlete, musician, or an elected official. But if your heart is set on going "raw dog," as they say on the street, then you're going to have to make sure that (A) your man is disease-free, and (B) you're the only woman he's with.

Take him to the clinic so both of you can get tested for HIV and every other STD. If he refuses to go, run. If he goes to the clinic and gets a clean bill of health, sit him down for a sober face-to-face conversation. Shine a big light directly into his eyes and ask him straight up: are you having sex, knocking boots, doing the nasty, getting it on, getting freaky-deaky, visiting the Piggly Wiggly, stroking the kitty-cat, digging a hole, hittin' it (I like to give a lot of options so the guy can't claim he doesn't know what I'm talking about) with anyone besides me? If he says you're the only one, you need to get him to put it in writing: have him send out a tweet that he, and his penis, are taken.

# "What do you mean you thought I was in a coma?"

## LONI LOVE'S TOP TEN REASONS MEN GIVE FOR SLEEPING WITH OTHER WOMEN

- "We were on a break."
- "I was out of town."
- "I didn't realize we were *both* supposed to be monogamous. I thought that was just you."
- "She's an ex and we've already slept together, so it's not really cheating."
- "She's a stripper. That counts?"
- "She's my boss's daughter."
- "Define 'having sex.'"
- "I lost a bet."
- "She looks just like you."
- "All the other guys were doing it."

*Dear Loni,*

*My man wants to have a threesome. Should I do it?*

*Signed,*
*One Is Never Enough*

Dear Enough,

I don't really understand the attraction of a threesome. That's just too many naked people for my taste. Plus, I've never found a bed big enough. But that's just me.

My friend Tamara's boyfriend asked her to have a threesome and she said yes. Her man was so happy, he thought, *She really is the woman of my dreams!* Well, guess what happened? Tamara and the other chick really hit it off. They hit it off so well they started seeing each other on the side. One thing led to another, and that's how Tamara lost a boyfriend and gained a girlfriend.

I'm just saying that sometimes threesomes get complicated. My advice to you is to set some ground rules. For instance, no friends, family, or coworkers allowed. You might even consider hiring a professional escort, because once you pay them, they leave.

> "No, I am not having a threesome with this waitress just because you want to eat dinner for free."

## LONI LOVE'S PROS AND CONS OF HAVING A THREESOME

| Pros | Cons |
| --- | --- |
| Meet new people | Meet sex-crazed lunatics |
| Find out what the cashier at the grocery store looks like naked | Find out what the cashier at the grocery store looks like naked |
| Explore your sexuality | Jealous rage |
| Learn you like new things in bed | Have to buy a bigger bed |
| Someone else can lie in the wet spot | You end up lying on the floor |
| You fulfill his fantasy | Now he thinks everything is fair game and asks to include your mom |
| Two mouths are better than one | Now you have to wait your turn |

*Dear Loni,*

*The guy I am dating has a tiny penis. Should I say something?*

> *Signed,*
> *Need More Friction*

Dear Need More,

Girl, one time I was dating a man and his penis was so small it could fit on a saltine cracker. It was the smallest penis in the world. In fact, you couldn't really call it a penis; it was just a bump. This man was a politician. He was smart and classy and I liked him, so I tried to make it work. But the fact is, sex is important in a relationship and I had a boyfriend who couldn't satisfy me. The love affair was doomed.

When I ended the romance, did I tell my boyfriend his joystick was the size of a Vienna sausage? No. Telling a man he has a small penis is just plain mean. He knows what size he is! He doesn't need you to point it out. The only man who needs to be told he has a tiny dick is the guy who just cut you off in traffic.

And besides, maybe his penis isn't that small. Maybe you just have an unusually roomy vagina. At least that's what your boyfriend is going to say after you tell him, "Your penis looks really small in those jeans." Now both of you will have hurt feelings and you'll be doing extra Kegel exercises trying to tighten up your Grand Canyon. I would leave this one alone.

# 3

# MOVING IN

*If you're like me*—an independent woman and queen of your castle—moving in with a boyfriend can be a huge adjustment and not a decision that should be made lightly. Even so, every day I hear about women rushing into cohabitation for all the wrong reasons. I know one woman who decided to shack up because she was scared to sleep alone. I told her, "Girl, you don't need a live-in boyfriend. You need a Rottweiler." Living together before you and your man are ready can lead to broken hearts, messy breakups, and your name on a lease you can't afford to pay on your own. Just like bungee jumping, before you move in you have to make sure you're ready to take the leap.

So how do you know if it's time for you and your honey to combine your closet space and share a tube of toothpaste? First, ask yourself the most basic question: *Am I willing to interact with this person every single day?* Remember, this doesn't mean seeing your boo only when he's showered and shaved and ready for a night on the town. It means enduring his early-morning stinky breath, gassy stomach, and head-in-the-toilet hangover. You'll have to put up with his farting in his sleep, belching at the dinner table, and acting like a baby when he gets a stuffy nose. And, of course, he's also going to see you when you're not looking like your most fly self. Think back to the last time you had the flu, or food poisoning, or even just a run-of-the-mill case of diarrhea. Are you ready to share all that with your soul mate?

Next you need to look at your current living situation and figure out if you're practically living together already. Do you and your man sleep in the same bed every night, or do you only get together when one of you wants sex? Do you sometimes have fun whipping up a dinner together from whatever you find in the fridge, or do you always eat out? Do you combine laundry and run it through the same wash, or has he never seen your dirty socks? Are your tampons on a shelf in his bathroom where anyone can see, or do you stash them in your purse? The way a couple sleeps, eats, and stores the tampons are all indicators of intimacy. If he's okay with your feminine products in his bathroom and you don't mind his sweaty gym clothes comingling with yours, you may both be ready to share the same address.

You should also examine how you and your boyfriend behave in an argument. Specifically, can the two of you disagree in close quarters without having law enforcement involved? Sure, it's easy to have a difference of opinion with someone when you're talking on the phone. You can roll your eyes, flip him the bird, and even put down the phone and grab a snack if the conversation isn't going the way you'd like. But when every disagreement gets hashed out in person, you really need to be on the same page when it comes to resolving conflict. For instance, some people like to get things off their chests. Let's call these folks "Yellers." Other folks like to retreat until things blow over. Let's call these people "Avoiders." What happens when you get a Yeller and an Avoider in the same house and they have an argument? The Yeller yells while the Avoider tries to lock himself in the bathroom. This is what I call a failure to communicate, aka a recipe for disaster.

Now it's time to ask yourself, *Do I like his sense of humor?* Not everyone factors humor into their living-together equation, but as a comedian I think life and love should be filled with laughter. This only happens if you live with someone with a similar sense of humor. If his idea of a good joke is passing gas at church and you're pretty sure this is breaking a commandment, then maybe you should just be friends.

And certainly you want to think about how you express your love. Some people are touchy-feely, others like to talk about their emotions, and still others express their love in less direct ways, like coming home every night (now that's my type of man!). You want to make sure that you and your man speak the same love language so you can hear him loud and clear when he tells you you're amazing. After all, the number one reason for moving in together is having someone tell you you're wonderful on a regular basis. If that's not happening, you might as well just get that Rottweiler.

# "Before I move in, you need to tell me why your apartment smells like cheese."

(Everything you need to know about shacking up, messy boyfriends, and what to do if you accidentally have sex with your roommate.)

*Dear Loni,*

*My boyfriend thinks we should move in together to save money. I love him but I'm just not sure. What do you think?*

*Signed,*
*On the Fence*

Dear On the Fence,

Right after college, my boyfriend Roscoe suggested the two of us move in together. He figured, why should we pay for two apartments when we're always together? I figured living with Roscoe would mean I'd have someone to rub my bunions every night, so I was all for it.

Well, it turns out the money I saved by only paying half the rent didn't even cover the increase in household bills. One day I came home to find Roscoe had used an entire container of Tide to wash a load of clothes. "I like to watch the bubbles!" he yelled as I smacked him with the empty bottle.

Not only did Roscoe do laundry like a five-year-old, he was a football player, so he ate like a horse. He would devour a jar of peanut butter, a dozen eggs, twelve biscuits, and fifteen links of sausage for breakfast. He ate so much we had to take out a loan from my mother to make ends meet. Borrowing money from Momma Love is no joke. She charges fifty cents on the dollar. She calls it "tough love." I call it being a loan shark.

Girl, don't make the same mistake I did. Before you move in together, do the math. Does your man leave the lights on all night because he's afraid of the dark? Does he blast the heat and the AC at the same time because he likes his warm air with a breeze? Does he use an entire roll every time he poops because he likes to cover the seat in toilet paper before he sits down, just like his momma taught him? If your man is going to cost you more money than you're paying now, keep your own place until you know for sure you're in it for keeps. Then make sure he gets you a Costco membership so you can buy plenty of toilet paper, laundry detergent, and all the seventy-five-pound jars of peanut butter his greedy ass can eat.

*Dear Loni,*

*I had sex with my roommate. Do you think this will impact our living arrangement?*

*Signed,*
*Too Close for Comfort*

Dear Too Close,

The only way getting it on with your roommate isn't going to affect your relationship is if the two of you were too drunk to remember it.

My friend Mimi slept with her roommate Jeffrey, and it didn't turn out so well. One night the two of them stayed up late, talking and drinking. Mimi suggested they play strip poker and before she knew it, she was the one getting poked. The two of them never had sex again and everything was fine until Jeffrey started dating Sally or, as Mimi calls her, "that ho."

Even though Mimi tried to act as though having sex with Jeffrey was no big deal, she couldn't stand the idea of his being with someone else. One night, Mimi just snapped. She called Sally and screamed, "This is Mimi and I had sex with your boyfriend!" That's when Jeffrey moved out.

The point is, when a man and a woman (or a man and a man or a woman and a woman or a man and a blow-up doll) have sex, someone is bound to develop feelings. Well, maybe not the blow-up doll. You need to sit down with your roommate and have an honest talk about the situation. Do you want to pursue this relationship? Or do you both want to chalk it up to a onetime freak fest? Hopefully you both feel the same way. If not, you better pack your bags, call your sister, and tell her to get her couch and margarita machine ready for a visit.

## "Is that my toothbrush in your mouth?"

### LONI LOVE'S GUIDE TO THINGS YOU SHOULD NEVER DO WITH YOUR ROOMMATE

- Share underwear
- Compare body parts
- Have a threesome
- Save water by showering together
- Share a one-bedroom apartment with only one bed
- Have a naked pillow fight
- Rub his balls

*Dear Loni,*

*I just moved in with my boyfriend. While I was organizing a closet I found a stash of love letters from his ex-girlfriend. What should I do?*

> *Signed,*
> *Apparently NOT the Girl of His Dreams*

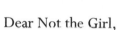

Dear Not the Girl,

Honey, this exact thing happened to me, only I was the ex-girlfriend!

Mike and I dated in college, and to this day we're still good friends. In fact, I'm even good friends with Mike's wife, T.J. One night they invited me over for dinner. After some delicious appetizers and a few cocktails, Mike and T.J. went into the kitchen to check on the dinner, leaving me alone in the living room. Now, I'm not one to snoop, but the mantel was covered in what looked like family photos I hadn't seen before, so I stepped over to take a closer look. There were pictures of the two of them on vacation in the Bahamas, some baby pictures of the kids, and in a gold frame was a picture of me and Mike from our college days. Back then Mike called me his "Chocolate Bunny"; I had an asymmetrical weave and I was forty pounds thinner. We were hugged up and looking like two peas in a pod.

I was horrified. Not only did I think it was disrespectful for him to have a picture of us mixed in with the family photos, the shoulder pads on my belly shirt looked ridiculous! So I grabbed the picture and tried to stuff it in my purse. That's when T. J. walked in and caught me. "What are you doing?" she asked. I guess she thought I was robbing her like my cousin Skillet does when anyone invites him over for dinner.

I told her I thought the picture of me and Mike might make her uncomfortable, so I was taking it back. She said, "Don't be ridiculous. You are a part of Mike's past and I respect that. We like that picture. Please put it back on the shelf." After she finished checking my purse for stolen silverware, we had a very nice dinner.

It's perfectly normal for a man to keep mementos of relationships that happened before he met you. As long as he keeps his love letters in a box in the back of his closet, you're okay. But if he keeps them in the same drawer as his baby oil, candles, and tissues, then you may have a problem.

# "Get out now, but leave the sofa."

## LONI LOVE'S LIVING-TOGETHER DEAL BREAKERS

- He brings home seven kids from the Little League team he coaches to play ball in the backyard. Then you realize they are all calling him "Dad."
- He asks you to squeeze that weird thing on his back.
- He says he knows the perfect place for the two of you to live: his mother's basement.
- He tells you, "*Mi casa es su casa*. Except on Thursday from seven to nine, when the masseuse comes over."
- You come home from a long day at work and find him drinking beer out of your $400 shoes.
- He tells you that in his culture the women pay all the bills as a sign of respect.

*Dear Loni,*

*My mother says if I move in with my boyfriend, he'll never marry me. Is she right?*

> *Signed,*
> *Boxes Are Packed*

Dear Packed,

Your mom doesn't want you shacking up with someone because you're her baby and she is trying to protect you. You know the saying "Why buy the cow when you can get the milk for free?" Your mother is trying to keep you from being a cow . . . a mad cow, that is.

If marriage is your goal, then your mom is right: you need to be very careful about moving in together, because once a girlfriend moves in, it's very easy for her to start acting like a wife. And if you play the role without a ring, you're in big trouble.

My friend Cathy had been dating Jim for two years when Jim suggested they move in together. Cathy thought living together would be a perfect way for her to show him how wonderful his life would be if the two of them got married. As soon as she moved in, Cathy went into "wife mode," cooking and cleaning and doing Jim's laundry. She spent all her social time with Jim's friends and family. She opened a joint bank account and tried sexual positions she had promised herself she would only do when she was married. After two years, it occurred to Cathy that maybe Jim hadn't proposed because he was getting the milk for free. So Cathy went on strike and started acting like a roommate instead of a spouse.

Cathy would make herself lavish dinners for one and hand Jim the stack of takeout menus. When Jim had a hard day at work, she would pretend to listen to him complain while texting her friends about what to wear to the club. When Jim's mom came over for a visit, Cathy would leave. After three months of Cathy's friend-with-no-benefits behavior, Jim had had enough. He wanted his wifey back, but this time he knew he had to do it her way. He proposed, and now the two of them have been happily married for five years. The moral of the story is, if you want to be married, don't act like a wife until you've got that ring on your finger.

# "We've been together fifteen years; I'm still waiting for a ring."

## LONI LOVE'S SIGNS HE'S NOT LOOKING FOR A WIFE

- You live together but you still don't have a key to the mailbox.
- He won't tell you his middle name.
- At your best friend's wedding, he tackles you to the ground to keep you from catching the bouquet.
- You have two children together but he says he doesn't want to "rush into anything."
- He throws himself a huge birthday party and doesn't invite you.

*Dear Loni,*

*I moved in with my boyfriend only to discover he's a total slob. How can I get him to change?*

> *Signed,*
> *Disgusted*

Dear Disgusted,

Sweetie, as Momma Love says, there is not a man on the face of this earth who will change until he is good and ready. That's just the way men are. If your boyfriend is a slob, he will always be a slob. If you are going to live with him, you are going to have to clean up after his sloppy ass.

> ## "I know you're a fan, but do you have to wear that giant wedge of cheese on your head?"

### LONI LOVE'S GUIDE TO THINGS YOU CAN'T STOP A MAN FROM DOING (NO MATTER HOW MUCH THEY ANNOY YOU)

- Collecting comic books, even though he's forty-seven
- Calling you over like he has something important to say and then farting loudly and laughing
- Taking advice from his best friend, the one you call The Idiot
- Standing in line for five hours at the Apple Store to buy the latest iPhone, even though he's still paying for his last one
- Wearing his high school gym shorts to go jogging because he insists they still fit
- Asking you to admire the poop he just made because he thinks it looks exactly like Abraham Lincoln
- Demanding you address his penis as "King Henry the First"

*Dear Loni,*

*My boyfriend and I used to have crazy wild sex all the time. But now that we live together it's the same old same old. How can I bring the excitement back?*

*Signed,*
*Bored in Bed*

Dear Bored,

When I get bored with sex I just add more liquor. If that doesn't work for you, you might need a Sex Night Extreme Makeover.

Get creative, girl! Go to the costume store and buy yourself a platinum-blond wig and a tight dress and greet your man at the door as Marilyn Monroe or Nicki Minaj or SpongeBob SquarePants, if that's what he's into. (I'm not judging.) Playing dress-up is the quickest way to spice things up. You just have to be careful.

One time I wanted to surprise my boyfriend Roscoe, so I bought a BeDazzler kit to jazz up my vajayjay. I glued on so many feathers and sparkles and sprinkled on so much glitter my crotch looked like an extra from the movie *Showgirls*. Ten years later, I'm still finding feathers stuck to my ass.

# "No, I'm not making an ice-cream sundae in the bedroom. The whipped cream is for you."

## LONI LOVE'S GUIDE TO KEEPING IT SEXY

| Do | Don't |
| --- | --- |
| Write your man flirty notes telling him what you have planned for him when he comes home. | Leave him a list of chores on his pillow. |
| Tell him he's the sexiest man you've ever laid eyes on. | Tell him he would be sexy if he was taller and had a different personality. |
| Wear sexy lingerie. | Wear lingerie that fitted you twenty-five pounds ago. |
| Shower together. | Wear a shower cap. |
| Pick him up at work in nothing but a trench coat and heels. | Get arrested for indecent exposure. |

*Dear Loni,*

*I love my boyfriend, but I need my alone time. When we move in together, can I still keep my own place so I can have somewhere to go to be by myself?*

*Signed,*
*Me Time*

Dear Me Time,

Of course you can keep your own place, but unless you have Oprah money I can't see why you would pay for an apartment you're not living in full-time. Back in the day, when I needed alone time from my live-in Roscoe, I would head to the public library. I'd find a corner table with my name on it, put my head down, and sleep. When I woke up, I was refreshed and ready to argue.

There are plenty of free places to get some alone time. You can go to a bed store and take a nap in the window display, find a really tall building and ride the elevator up and down, or go to a funeral parlor and tell them you'd like to test out some caskets. If you want to get fancy you can even rent a hotel room. But whatever you do, stay away from places, like the Sweet Foxy Motel, that charge by the hour.

*Dear Loni,*

*My boyfriend and I have been living together for two weeks and I have yet to see him totally naked. He always has a towel wrapped around him, or he's under the sheets, or the lights are out. How do I get him to be more open with me?*

*Signed,*
*Wonder What He's Hiding*

Dear Wonder,

I feel where your boyfriend is coming from. When I first moved in with Roscoe, I would keep a towel around me at all times. I even put a stack of extra towels by the side of the bed so I could grab one and cover myself whenever I needed to run to the kitchen for a snack. Well, that lasted about two weeks. I got tired of doing all that laundry. Plus, Roscoe had used all the Tide.

Your boyfriend is probably just shy. If you really want to check out his goodies, make him a double martini and wait until he passes out. Then you can look all you want. But you probably won't need to do all that. Now that you two live together, I doubt your boyfriend is going to keep up the modesty, no matter how shy he is. Sooner or later, people need to let their Wild Kingdom roam free! In fact, a few weeks after Roscoe and I moved in together he came home with a guest to find me relaxing on the back porch, sipping a giant pink margarita and sunbathing in the nude. You should have seen the look on his mother's face.

*Dear Loni,*

*I found my boyfriend's stash of porn on his computer. We have a good sex life. Why does he want to watch other women have sex?*

*Signed,*
*Not a Porn Star*

Dear Porn Star,

From pastors and politicians to the average Joe, almost all men watch a little porn from time to time. But some men go overboard. My friend Ralph loves porn so much that it's impossible for him to be in a normal relationship. He expects every woman he dates to have implants, love anal sex, and come with a "boom-chicka-waah-waah" soundtrack that plays every time she enters the room.

You need to figure out if your man is like Ralph. Does your boyfriend watch porn instead of making love to you? Does he watch porn *while* making love to you? Does he use porn like an instructional video, pointing at the screen and telling you, "Notice her perfect form. That's how it's done!"?

If your man's porn viewing is interfering with your relationship, then tell him it bothers you and see if you can come to some kind of agreement. If your boyfriend has a secret stash that he watches when he's alone, it might be one of those things you choose to let slide. Just keep his computer away from the kids. You don't want to have to explain why that nice lady is naked with a ball gag in her mouth.

# "No, your mother may not sleep in the bed with us."

## LONI LOVE'S HOUSE RULES FOR LIVING HAPPILY EVER AFTER

- No strip poker on family game night.
- No tipping the babysitter with sex.
- No spanking (unless I ask for it).
- No watching porn while we're eating dinner.
- No watching porn while we're eating breakfast.
- No using the cucumber from our "try something new" sex night in the dinner salad.
- No sharing underwear, unless someone forgets to do the laundry.

# 4

# BREAKING UP

*A lot of women think* that once they get into a good relationship all their problems will go away. But even good relationships have their ups and downs. It's perfectly normal to be madly in love with a man and then one day find yourself ticked off by the sound of him eating his cornflakes. Suddenly you're thinking, *Do you really have to slurp your milk like that? You sound like a wild pig.* This is what I like to call temporary man-induced irritation.

If you've ever been in a long-term relationship, you're probably very familiar with this condition. It's the feeling you get when you look at your man and think, *If you leave your wet towel on the bathroom floor again I'm moving out,* or *I am not going anywhere with you dressed in those bike shorts,* or *Is that smell coming from you?* But getting past these irritations, and buying your man new clothes, are what keeps a relationship strong.

What is not okay, however, is being in a relationship that is in a slow decline with no chance of ever getting better.

It's not okay to feel so frustrated with your situation that you update your Facebook status to "fucked up." It's not okay to be married and wonder if it's too late to become a nun. It's not okay to look at your man and think to yourself, *I don't trust you, your friends, your momma, or your dog.* Even so, plenty of women know their relationships are over but refuse to leave. In fact, they often have all kinds of excuses for why they should stay, like they're afraid of hurting their man's feelings, or they're scared of growing old alone, or they still owe his mother some money. Honey, I'm here to tell you, if you go to sleep silently praying that your man will move out in the middle of the night, it's time to let go.

One of the first signs your relationship is in trouble is when you no longer feel sexually attracted to your man. Desire is critical to the success of any long-lasting relationship, but sometimes the flame just peters out. Maybe your man let himself go, and you just don't find his new giant beer belly and untrimmed pubic hair attractive. Or maybe you never found him all that sexy to begin with, and the passage of time has only made things worse. Whatever the reason for your lack of lust, before you dump your boo in the hopes of hooking up with the sexy FedEx delivery guy, you need to figure out if this is a permanent problem or one that can be solved by your man taking his fat ass to the gym. Close your eyes and imagine your partner looking the way he did when you first met him. Now give him a passionate kiss on the lips. Feel anything? No, nothing? Girl, it's time for you to go.

Another sign it's time to end the relationship is when you find yourself so filled with rage you don't even feel like yourself anymore. This usually happens when the man does something that makes you angry, like throwing up in your brand-new car. Only instead of working to repair the relationship (and your car), you are consumed with thoughts of revenge. How do you know if you're in this situation?

Easy. Are you excited when your man gets a ride to work and leaves his Toyota at home, because it will give you a chance to put sugar in his gas tank? This is not a relationship, it's war. Get out now.

The last sign that it's time to call it quits is when you find yourself doing things to sabotage your relationship. Your strategy is, if he catches me, he'll dump me and then I'll be free. But being too afraid to break up with your boyfriend is not a good reason to sleep with his boss. Plus, this is not grown-woman behavior. If you want out of your relationship, woman up and get out! Don't create a lot of drama just so he can be the one to end it. It's not fair to him, it's not good for you, and you're better than that. Girl, I know getting out of a relationship can be difficult. It takes courage to leave a situation knowing you'll be on your own for a while. But think of how wonderful life will be when you don't have to wake up every morning, roll over to look at your man, and think, *Why are you still here?*

# "It's not you . . . okay, I lied, it *is* you."

(Everything you need to know about breaking up, moving on, and what to do about the ex who won't take his stuff and get out of your place.)

Dear Loni,

*Two years ago, my boyfriend moved into my place. Now we're breaking up, but my ex refuses to move out. How do I get him to leave?*

> Signed,
> Name on the Lease

Dear Lease,

Oh, girl, I had this exact problem with my ex-boyfriend Clarence. Clarence and I had been dating for a year when we decided to take it to the next level by moving in together. For a while it was paradise: we cooked together, watched movies, and had sex without having to plan for it. But then came trouble.

Living together meant we had bills to pay. But Clarence seemed to think they would magically pay themselves while he decided whether to pursue his dream of becoming a professional carpet cleaner, a rapper, or, if you can believe it, my manager. Clarence would come to my open-mic nights and give me notes on my performance. One night, Clarence said I reminded him of a black Lucille Ball, then handed me a bright red wig. That was the last straw. I didn't need to live with a freeloader, especially one who was trying to tell me how to run my career.

I told Clarence he had a month to get his stuff and get out. Clarence looked me up and down, puffed out his chest, and said, "I'm not going nowhere." And then it was war. Clarence wasn't leaving and I wasn't about to let him stay. Hell, he had moved into *my* apartment! I was pissed, and when I get angry I tap into my alter ego, Detroit Debbie. She's tough, rough, and can handle any stuff.

One day Clarence left the house to hang out with his boys at the barbershop. While he was gone, Debbie got to work. She removed all the food from the apartment, shut off the electricity, and turned all the furniture upside down so Clarence wouldn't have anywhere to sit. When Clarence got home, he opened the door, then tripped over the upside-down sofa. "Did we get robbed?" he asked, dismayed. "No," I said. "But you need to leave."

Drastic situations call for drastic measures. Tap into your Detroit Debbie and tell your man his time is up.

*Dear Loni,*

*My boyfriend dumped me and I can't stop thinking about him. How can I get over my ex and move on?*

*Signed,*
*Heartbroken*

Dear Heartbroken,

Momma Love says there is only one thing that will mend a broken heart, and that's time. I suggest you get a wall calendar, count exactly six months forward, and draw a smiley face on that day. I promise, by the time you get to the happy face you won't feel as bad as you do now. But that doesn't mean you should pass the time sitting at home staring at old pictures of you and your ex playing Frisbee on the beach, tearing it up at the nightclub, or making new friends at your AA meetings. You need to keep yourself busy.

When my friend Heather broke up with her ex, she decided to do something adventurous, so she signed up for flight classes to learn how to fly a plane. Heather was such an enthusiastic student that she started dating the flying instructor, who, lucky for her, looked just like Denzel Washington. Now he flies her wherever she wants to go. I was so inspired when I saw how much fun Heather was having with her new boyfriend that I signed up for classes too. The problem was instead of a Denzel-looking pilot, my instructor ended up being a toothless World War II vet named Wilbur. The only place he wanted to take me was the early-bird special at the Happy Valley Senior Center, and I always had to pick up the tab.

*Dear Loni,*

*I've been living with my boyfriend for three weeks. Yesterday I came home to find a life-sized poster of Beyoncé hanging over the bed. My boyfriend says Beyoncé "inspires" him. I tried to tell him I don't want a poster of a beautiful woman hanging in the bedroom but my boyfriend refuses to take it down. Now I'm worried I made a horrible mistake by moving in. I think maybe we should break up. What do you think?*

*Signed,*
*Not Liking His Decorating*
*Choices*

Dear Choices,

For some men, "home décor" means decorating like they live in a frat house. My ex Clarence is one of these guys. Clarence is a huge basketball fan. One day I came home to find a six-foot poster of LeBron James hanging on the wall across from our bed. LeBron was sweaty and glistening, and looking fine as hell! When things between me and Clarence weren't going too well in bed, I would fantasize that LeBron was making love to me. This worked out fine until one night when Clarence was on top of me huffing and puffing and I called out, "Oh, LeBron, slam-dunk me, baby!" This shook Clarence so badly, the very next day he took down his poster.

Girl, you don't need to end your relationship over a poster of Beyoncé. You just need to fight fire with fire. Become a huge fan of LeBron James and hang up your own damn poster.

Dear Loni,

*I snooped on my fiancé and found out he has an active profile on an online dating website. What should I do?*

Signed,
*I Thought We Were Exclusive*

Dear Exclusive,

Okay, let's be real here. If your fiancé has an online dating profile, he's either cheating or about to. My friend Stephanie was dating a man she thought was perfect. He was funny, he was generous, and he knew how to fix her leaking kitchen faucet. One night he was using her computer to check his e-mail. When he got up to go to the bathroom, Stephanie jumped at her chance to snoop. Now, I don't know if snooping is always the right thing to do (I wouldn't want anyone going through my search history of "buffets in every state," "plus-size sex toys," and "fun ways to use zucchini"). But I do know this: women have powers of intuition. If your gut tells you you should snoop, there's probably something you need to know.

Stephanie searched through her man's e-mail and discovered dozens of messages from a woman he used to date. Clearly, the romance was not over. By the time her boyfriend came out of the bathroom, Stephanie had decided to dump his ass. She said later, "Seeing his e-mail gave me all the information I needed. He's a cheater and I can do better."

You now have all the information *you* need about your fiancé to make a decision. Do you want to marry a man who acts like he's still single? Or do you want a relationship with someone who you can let use your computer without worrying about an instant message from PlentyofAss.com?

## "Is this an invitation to your wedding? Because I thought you and I were still dating."

### LONI LOVE'S GUIDE TO KNOWING WHEN THE RELATIONSHIP IS REALLY OVER

- He thinks it's okay that you only see him at work.
- He introduces you to his kids and tells them you're the nice cleaning lady.
- He counts bumping into him at Starbucks as a date.
- He asks your opinion of the naked picture he just took of himself before he tweets it to his "friend."
- You see him on the street and he turns around and starts running in the other direction.
- His mother asks if you've met his new girlfriend.
- He files a police report calling you a stalker.

*Dear Loni,*

*I want to break up with my boyfriend, but I think he's going to take it really hard. How do I let him down easy?*

> *Signed,*
> *Feeling Guilty*

Dear Guilty,

No one likes to break another person's heart. That's why God invented the phrase "It's not you, it's me." The problem is, everybody knows that line is a crock. If I am breaking up with you, it *is* you! If I thought you were perfect, I wouldn't be leaving. Still, telling a man all the reasons he doesn't measure up is unnecessary. A nicer way to break up with someone is to give him as few details as possible. People need to know the truth, but not necessarily the *whole* truth. This strategy has worked wonders for me.

Toward the end of my relationship with Clarence I was no longer attracted to him. Did I tell him he was beginning to remind me of Wilbur, the World War II vet I dated briefly? Of course not. I didn't want to have to pick up the pieces of Clarence's shattered ego. Instead, I looked him dead in the eye and said, "Clarence, I care about you but I know you can do so much better." He thought I was saying he could do better than me. Really, I was talking about his raggedy-ass suit.

# "It's not you. It's your mother."

## LONI LOVE'S GUIDE TO LETTING HIM DOWN EASY

| The real problem | What to tell him |
| --- | --- |
| He's not ambitious enough. | "It's wonderful how you've never changed." |
| He has BO. | "You smell like a rock star!" |
| You don't want to have his children. | "I would be a terrible mother." |
| He's really, really dumb. | "It's amazing how your parents look so much alike... almost as if they are related." |
| He's gained fifty pounds. | "You're so jolly, I would only bring you down." |
| His poor hygiene has your apartment smelling like an elephant sanctuary. | "I don't want to hold you back; you should be free... in the wild." |
| You like his brother more than you like him. | "I don't deserve you. I deserve someone *like* you. But definitely not you." |

*Dear Loni,*

*My boyfriend and I broke up three months ago. Ever since, he's been dropping by and we've been having sex. I miss him but it's making me crazy! What should I do?*

> *Signed,*
> *Need to Close Up Shop*

Dear Shop,

Women are emotional creatures (or, as some men like to say, "crazy"). So unless you're a sexual free spirit (or, as some women like to say, "a skank"), it's going to be difficult for you to have sex without feeling a connection to the person you are with. Sex with your ex is especially difficult because it puts you in a no-man's-land: you're not together, but you're not apart either. And you certainly can't move on to someone new.

For men, it's a whole different story. When it comes to sex, most men can multitask. A dude can have sex with his ex, date a new girl, hook up with his high school sweetheart, and sleep with his kid's second-grade teacher all in the same afternoon. And if you're on his roster, you don't know if you are the main piece, the side piece, or part of a three-piece.

You're right; it is time for you to close up shop. You know what that means: block him on all your social media sites. Stop answering his texts. Replace his name in your phone with "do not answer," or "he has a little penis," or "he's an idiot and his momma is too." Stop answering his calls and move on. There's a better guy out there waiting for you, one who's willing to do more than drop by for a quickie.

> ## "Please put your clothes back on. We broke up a month ago."

### LONI LOVE'S GUIDE TO THINGS YOU CAN'T DO WITH YOUR EX (NO MATTER HOW MUCH YOU MISS HIM)

- Clean his apartment
- Clean his mother's apartment
- Text him to wish him a happy birthday, then tell him you're standing on his doorstep naked
- Help him shop for lingerie for his new girlfriend and insist you try it on
- Have sex with him behind the church the morning of his wedding in a desperate attempt to get him to change his mind

*Dear Loni,*

*My ex and I broke up three weeks ago and now he's spying on me. I found him hiding in the bushes outside my house last week, peering into my living room window. What should I do?*

*Signed,*
*On Stalker Alert*

Dear Alert,

Girl, if your man is acting crazy, which it sounds like he is, the first thing you need to do is call the police and file a report. It is not cute when an ex starts acting like a member of the paparazzi. You should also get a guard dog and, if you can, a new boyfriend who's bigger than your ex.

One night a few weeks after we broke up, I caught Clarence looking into my bedroom window, which was really strange since I lived on the fourth floor. I flung open the window and asked what the hell he was doing. He said he was checking to see if he left his sneakers. He said he didn't want to bother me by ringing the doorbell, like a normal person. So instead he borrowed the neighbor's ladder, climbed onto the roof, shinnied down the waterspout, and balanced on a two-inch-wide beam to look in the window. "Clarence," I said, "you know damn well you were spying on me." I was not happy, and neither was my date, Wilbur. Wilbur might have been old, but he knew how to shoot.

If you are worried about your ex, you need to make like Goldilocks and go to the forest. Dig up a big batch of poison ivy and plant it all around your house. The next time you see your man sneaking around your place, let him spend a good while crouched in the bushes, then call the cops. You'll give him an itchy night in the holding cell he'll never forget.

*Dear Loni,*

*My husband and I broke up six months ago, but his mom still calls me every Sunday. How do I end the relationship with his mother?*

*Signed,*
*Not a Momma's Girl*

Dear Girl,

As difficult as it is to break up with a man, if you have developed a relationship with his mother it's even harder to break up with *her*.

When I was dating Clarence, I got very close with his mother, Miss Alice. I would go over to Miss Alice's house every Sunday to keep her company. We would watch the game, go shopping, and even go to church. I was like the daughter she never had. And Miss Alice could cook! I fell in love with her the minute she served me my favorite, liver and onions. When Clarence and I broke up, I didn't want to break up with Miss Alice's cooking, so I tried for as long as I could to keep the relationship going. The problem was Miss Alice kept trying to get me and Clarence back together.

Every weekend, she would invite me to dinner and Clarence would show up. Miss Alice would putter around, lighting dinner candles and pouring grape juice (which I would "refresh" with a little Wild Turkey in the powder room). Then, just as we were all sitting down to eat, Miss Alice would suddenly announce that she had completely forgotten she had somewhere she was supposed to be, like Bible study, or the Laundromat, or the zoo, leaving me and my ex to enjoy a romantic dinner alone. Once I caught on to her, I would bring my Tupperware. As soon as Miss Alice left, I would pack up my food and go.

Older women can be very emotional. You need to ease your ex's mother out of your life gradually. If she's been calling you every Sunday, let a Sunday go by without returning her call. Soon you'll be on an every-other-week phone-call plan. Then you can try getting her down to once a month. In about ten years, she'll be out of your life forever.

"I'm not dating your brother anymore, so stop asking if you can borrow six dollars."

## LONI LOVE'S GUIDE TO LETTING HIS FRIENDS AND RELATIVES KNOW IT'S OVER

- Tell his gossipy cousin; it will be all over town before you have time to change your Facebook status.
- Send out mass e-mails, texts, and postcards; organize a telephone tree; take out an ad in the local paper; and hire a small-engine aircraft to skywrite the message "It's over and I'm dating someone else."
- Host a weekly podcast called *Me and My New Boo*.
- Mail Christmas cards to his family with a picture of you and your new man wearing matching reindeer sweaters.
- Marry your new man.

*Dear Loni,*

*My boyfriend wants me to lose fifteen pounds. He says there is no way we can get married unless I trim down. I love my man, but I like how I look. Is this a deal breaker?*

*Signed,*
*Bootylicious*

Dear Booty,

I once had a boyfriend who told me he didn't want a fat wife. Hell, I was fat when he met me! So I told him I didn't want a broke husband. And that was the end of our relationship.

I don't know why men always think women are so desperate that we're willing to change for them. If you want to lose weight for you, that's one thing. But if your man doesn't accept you as you are, you need to find someone else who will. After my breakup with Mr. I Don't Want a Fat Wife, I decided to focus my energy on improving my career. That's when I decided to leave my job as an engineer and pursue my dream of becoming a stand-up comedian. Now I meet plenty of men who accept me for me, and I'm laughing while doing it. If your man thinks he'd like you better if you lost a few pounds, let him see how he likes it if you leave his ass and disappear completely.

*Dear Loni,*

*I met a guy, BigBoy69, on an online dating site and we really
hit it off! We've never met in person, but we chat online for hours.
The problem is, recently I've started a new romance with Wild-
man2013. We've been tweeting back and forth and I think he
might be my soul mate. How do I break up with BigBoy so I can
move on?*

*Signed,*
*One-Man Woman*

Dear Woman,

Sweetie, I hate to break it to you, but these are not
relationships. In fact, you don't even know if BigBoy and
Wildman are who they say they are. They might be doing
what we call "catfishing," pretending online to be someone
they are not. For all you know, they could be teenage boys, or
tween girls, or farm animals with Internet access.

My friend Ralph met a woman online. Natalie lived in
London, but Ralph was so convinced she was his soul mate
that he saved his money until he had enough to fly her to Los
Angeles. I tried to tell Ralph this was a horrible idea, but he

wouldn't listen. On the day Natalie was scheduled to arrive, I drove Ralph to the airport. (Ralph doesn't have a license. It got taken away after he racked up $5,075 in parking tickets from the time he got so drunk he forgot where he left his car and it took him two weeks to find it. These days Ralph gets around by city bus or his mobility scooter.)

When Natalie got off the plane, I could see by the look on her face she was stunned to discover that Ralph weighed 450 pounds. It didn't help that he also lived in a studio apartment in the 'hood and worked in a grocery store. Natalie arrived on a Friday morning and left Friday afternoon. Ralph could have saved himself a lot of money and hurt feelings if he had been truthful with Natalie in the first place and not sent her pictures of his face Photoshopped onto Channing Tatum's body.

I say you ditch both of these fake relationships and start something new. You can find a man on your favorite dating website, but limit yourself to a maximum of three online exchanges before moving the relationship into the real world. That means a face-to-face date. If the man isn't ready to have a relationship in the flesh, then he's wasting your time. And if you're interested in Ralph, just let me know.

# 5

# MAKING UP

*Girlfriends, have you ever* broken up with a guy and then wondered if maybe you made a mistake? I find breakup regret hits hardest when I'm on a bad first date with someone new, like the time I went out with the guy from ChristianMingle.com who spent the night misquoting scripture. But that twinge of regret can also strike if you suddenly see your ex walking down the street hand in hand with a Halle Berry look-alike. Or you might catch a case of second thoughts when you've spent your fifth Saturday night in a row at home alone, reminiscing about him leaving the toilet seat up.

Ladies, beware of breakup regret! Remember, you dumped this guy for a reason. Nothing's changed just because he has a hot new girlfriend. Maybe his new chick likes guys who lie on the sofa all day eating Cheetos and farting. You don't know the inner workings of their romance. But as much as I warn women against going back to the same old guy hoping for something new, I realize there are some relationships that *do* deserve a do-over.

The first reason to give a guy a second chance is what I like to call Circumstantial Evidence, meaning you have evidence that the circumstances of his life have changed for the better. Let's say, for instance, that you broke up with your ex because one day you looked at him and thought, *You can never give me the kind of life I want. Our future together looks bleak and possibly filled with legal bills.* In that case, you might consider giving your ex a second chance once he gets a job, or a better job, or wins the lottery, or the criminal charges against him are dropped. What you're looking for is a sign that says life with this man is going to be better than it was before. If you can see a bright and stable future for the two of you where previously you did not, then you have a green light to give this romance a second chance.

Another good reason to consider reconciliation is what I call Human Error. Human Error is when you realize that you were wrong about the reason you broke up with him in the first place. Maybe you thought he missed your cousin's art gallery opening on purpose and it turns out he worked a double shift that night so he could make some extra money to buy one of your cousin's beautiful macramé wall hangings. Or maybe you thought he was lying when he said he really didn't know how those pictures of naked double-D breasts got on his cell phone and then his wack-ass cousin confessed he did it as a joke. In short, you made a mistake, and getting back together is your way of saying, "My bad. Let's try this again."

The third reason to get back together with a man you've already broken up with is if he's committed to improving your relationship. I call this reason Signs of Change. Let's say you dump your ex because he's too critical. Then, after you break up, he suddenly starts sending you flowers and love letters telling you all the things he misses about you. Well, you might want to investigate his new attitude further. I'm not saying he's definitely a changed man. But I am saying you probably won't forgive yourself if you don't find out for sure.

Of course, all this comes with a caveat: if you're going to break up and get back together, you can only do it once. I repeat, you can only get back together once! Any more than that and he'll think you're a pushover, which only invites bad behavior. He'll be tempted to see how far he can take his shenanigans before you break up with him for real. Save yourself the trouble and dump his ass now. As Momma Love used to say, there's no point in leading a horse to water if he's only going to kick you in the damn face.

# "If I knew the makeup sex was going to be so good, I would have dumped you years ago."

(Everything you need to know about forgiving, forgetting, and repairing the relationship, even when *you* are the one who messed up.)

*Dear Loni,*

*I cheated on my boyfriend and we broke up for a while, but now we're back together. For a few weeks everything was fine but lately he's been making remarks that make me think he still feels bad about what happened. What can I do to get him to trust me again?*

*Signed,*
*I Cheated, Now What?*

Dear Cheated,

It's very hard for men to get over infidelity. I know because when my friend Zena cheated on her then-boyfriend, Kevin, he was so mad he made a video of the two of them having sex. He called the video *Zena: Queen of the Hos* and put it up on the Web. It turns out Kevin is a very talented filmmaker. The video went viral and now that Zena and Kevin are married, the video is still causing problems. They'll be at Applebee's and someone will recognize Zena, call her queen of the hos, and ask for an autograph. It's awkward. Especially for their children.

If you want your man to trust you, you are going to have to remind him over and over and over again how fantastic you think he is, what a great lover he is, and how much you admire his intellect. Once his ego is inflated to the size of Mount Olympus, he won't worry that you might still be cheating on him (but he may be impossible to live with).

# "Okay, okay, I'll have a threesome with the hot neighbor."

## LONI LOVE'S TIPS FOR GETTING YOUR MAN TO FALL IN LOVE WITH YOU ALL OVER AGAIN

- Cook his favorite meal.
- Cook his favorite meal naked.
- Say yes to that weird sex position he's been wanting to try.
- Do that weird sex position again, but this time don't complain about it.
- Give him pocket money for a night at a sports bar with his boys even though you suspect they're really going to the strip club.
- Praise him to his mother *and* his baby's mother.

*Dear Loni,*

*My boyfriend and I just got back together after being broken up for a year. The problem is, while we were apart he gained fifty pounds. How do I let him know I liked him better before?*

> *Signed,*
> *Like My Man with Less Meat on His Bones*

Dear Bones,

Girl, you are on some thin ice. Trying to tell a man what you don't like about him is never a good idea.

My friend T.J. thought she was being slick when she decided to tell her husband, Mike, that he needed to hit the gym. T.J. announced, "I'll just get him to play a game where we each say three things we would like to change about the other person." She figured Mike would tell her she was perfect and then, when it was her turn, she would tell him he would be perfect too, if only he would turn his keg into a six-pack. Was she surprised when it turned out that Mike had a long list of things he wanted T.J. to change: he asked her to scrub her ashy elbows, trim the bush, and file her toenails, which he called "bear claws." He also mentioned that he didn't particularly like her new hair color and thought a chin implant would greatly improve her profile. By the time

Mike had finished talking, T.J. was so upset she didn't even tell him about his flabby stomach. She just cleaned up the plate of spaghetti she had thrown at him and went to their bedroom to start working on her elbows.

Trust me, the best way to tell a man what's wrong with him is to let him figure it out for himself. So if your man has gained weight, buy him a pair of pants two sizes too small. Cut out the tag and replace it with a tag in his size. Then tell him you can't wait to see how hot he's going to look in his new threads. As you watch him struggling to get those pants over his ass, just shake your head sadly and walk out of the room. He'll get the message.

# "You'd be perfect if only you were completely different."

## LONI LOVE'S GUIDE TO TELLING YOUR MAN YOU WANT HIM TO CHANGE

| If you want him to ... | Tell him ... |
| --- | --- |
| dress better | "Shirts with sleeves turn me on!" |
| smell better | "Something about a good cologne makes me want to do really nasty things in bed." |
| do more housework | "I'm going to ask my mother to come over and help me tidy up." |
| make more money | "If we had more money, I would build myself a craft room and stay in there doing decoupage all weekend, especially during football season." |
| buy you more gifts | "I just read an article that says women give the most mind-blowing oral sex after they've received jewelry. I wonder if it's true." |

*Dear Loni,*

*My boyfriend always wants to have makeup sex after we fight, but I think he's just picking fights to have sex. How do I get him to stop?*

*Signed,*
*Lover Not a Fighter*

Dear Lover,

My ex Jamal also used to think sex was more exciting after a heated argument. To piss me off, he would snatch off my wig, or throw all the ice in the sink so I wouldn't have any to cool my adult beverage, or erase the episodes of Dr. Drew's *Celebrity Rehab* I had saved on the DVR. Instead of having five minutes of great sex and then watching an hour of TV (the way it's *supposed* to be), we would have an hour-long argument and then five minutes of crappy sex. It was a waste of my time.

Finally, I decided the fighting had to stop and came up with a plan: I started wearing sewn-in weaves so he couldn't pull off my hair, I learned to appreciate the taste of room-temperature Hennessy, and I waited for a marathon of *Celebrity Rehab* to get my fix of my boo Dr. Drew. In other words, I refused to let Jamal get me upset. Soon enough he realized that the sex was just as good, and maybe even better, when I had a smile on my face.

You need to show your man that an argument is not foreplay. Stop fighting and start loving.

> ## "I am not having makeup sex with you just because you gave me back the remote when I asked for it."

### LONI LOVE'S SILLY REASONS MEN GIVE TO HAVE MAKEUP SEX

| You're mad because ... | He suggests makeup sex to ... |
| --- | --- |
| he owes you money | pay you back |
| you've been at work all day, while he was at home lying on the sofa eating Cheetos | demonstrate that he was conserving his energy for sex |
| you checked his phone and saw he made a call to his ex | make sure you hear him scream your name (instead of hers) |
| he went to a strip club | prove Sparkle didn't give him a happy ending |

*Dear Loni,*

*My ex-boyfriend and I recently started seeing each other again, but while we were broken up I did a lot of things. And when I say, "a lot of things," I mean "a lot of guys." Should I confess now, or cross my fingers and hope he never finds out?*

*Signed,*
*Sowed My Oats, and Then*
*Some*

Dear Oats,

Honey, leave the confessions for the Dr. Phil show. This is real life and you should keep your mouth shut.

Now, I'm sure you chowed down on your man buffet because you were lonely and missing your boyfriend. And if your man ever finds out, I suggest that's exactly what you tell him. But hopefully, he won't find out, and you won't need to tell him anything at all. Still, if I were you, I'd see my doctor for a checkup. If not, you could end up like my friend Tammy.

A while ago, Tammy and her man had a big fight over Tammy's being a horrible cook. She was so mad she ended the relationship. A few nights later, Tammy got lonely and hungry (she really can't cook), so she went to IHOP for some midnight pancakes. While she was there, Tammy started flirting with the man at the next table. One thing led to another and the two of them ended up having a crazy syrup-filled one-night stand in the backseat of her car. A few days later, Tammy's ex called her to apologize and the two of them got back together. Her boyfriend would have been none the wiser, except IHOP dude had gifted Tammy with a terrible case of crabs—which she gave to her man. Tammy tried to pass it off by saying she picked up the bugs at culinary school. "It was part of a recipe!" she insisted. But her man wasn't buying it and they had to break up all over again.

What you did while you were broken up really isn't any of your man's business. You don't owe him a detailed account of your wild days without him, but you do owe him a clean vajayjay to come home to.

*Dear Loni,*

*My boyfriend and I are in a very tumultuous relationship. When we're together, we fight all the time. But as soon as we break up, we miss each other so much we get back together. My friends are getting sick of the drama and I can't blame them. What's wrong with me?*

*Signed,*
*Need a Ticket Out of Crazy Town*

Dear Crazy Town,

I don't blame your friends for being mad, either. They're probably tired of hearing you crying about your man one minute and seeing you make up with him the next. The question is, what's keeping you in this revolving-door romance? I'm going to take a wild guess and say that your childhood was a little chaotic. Maybe there was a lot of yelling, fighting, and slamming doors, so the drama with your man feels familiar to you. But that doesn't mean it's good for you.

When I was a little girl, my friend Denise would wait every Saturday morning for her dad to pick her up for a visit. Denise's apartment was on the first floor and I would pass by her window on my way out with my babysitter, Miss Brooks, who was a Jehovah's Witness. Miss Brooks's idea of taking care of me was to have me go door-to-door with her, spreading the good news of the Lord. All morning, as we walked around the housing complex getting doors slammed in our faces, I would keep my eye on Denise, sitting in the window, wearing her favorite dress with bows in her hair.

For years, Denise held out hope that her father would appear. Sometimes he would show up for his visits, sometimes he was late, and sometimes he wouldn't show up at all. By the time she reached high school, something in her snapped. I remember she said to me, "I am too fly to be waiting on any man. Even my father."

When she got to college, Denise started dating Roger, a wide receiver for the school football team. One time Roger was late to pick her up. After twenty minutes of waiting, with no phone call, Denise put on her coat and left her dorm room. She said, "I told you, I don't wait for any man." Later that night, while Denise was in the library studying, she heard wheezing sounds coming from the study cubicle next to her. It was a boy named Joel having an asthma attack. That's when Denise decided to become a doctor. Now Dr. Denise, Joel, and his inhaler are living happily ever after.

Denise had a choice: either keep waiting on men, the way she did with her father, or make a change and strive for something better, which is exactly what you should do. If you need some help, find a good therapist. Your friends might even help to pay.

*Dear Loni,*

*My boyfriend and I decided to take "a break" while we both went off to college. Now we are back together and planning to get married. The only problem is, I can't stop thinking about the guy I dated while we were on our break. What should I do?*

*Signed,*
*In a School Daze*

Dear School Daze,

Right before my ex Clarence asked me to move in with him, I got extremely cold feet and started to wonder if maybe I would be better off with Kilroy, who was also trying to date me at the time. As you can imagine, this happens to me constantly. Whenever I have to choose between men, I make a pros-and-cons list for both of them and see how they compare. I suggest you do the same.

Before you get married—and spend all that money on a dress, a bad wedding band, and feeding a bunch of people who are making side bets at the buffet on whether the marriage will last—you need to know if you are simply having engagement jitters or if you still have feelings for the other guy. Once you make the list, everything you need to know will be right there in front of your eyes.

"One has a big wallet, the other has a big love rocket. Life is full of difficult choices."

## LONI LOVE'S SELECTION PROCESS REVEALED*

| CLARENCE | | KILROY | |
|---|---|---|---|
| PRO | CON | PRO | CON |
| loves me | smothers me | likes me | likes a *lot* of women |
| is a hard worker | goes on frequent "business trips" and comes home with glitter in his suitcase | is still in college | expects me to pay for college |
| has a car | fights with me over the parking space | has a bus pass | I don't take the bus |
| supports my goals | tries to manage my career | writes jokes for me | the jokes are terrible |
| has no kids | wants kids | has no kids | acts like one |
| likes to have sex | lasts about five minutes | likes to have sex | lasts about three minutes |

*The winner was Clarence. Those extra two minutes in bed were important to me!

*Dear Loni,*

*My boyfriend and I have reconnected after a year apart. I'm happy we're back together, but he's changed. He's discovered yoga and has become a vegan. How can I get back the barbecue-eating man I love?*

*Signed,*
*Tired of Eating Alone*

Dear Tired,

Girl, I know just how you feel about meat. One time my friend Ricky invited me to a vegetarian barbecue. I only went to see what he was putting on the grill. It was a waste of my time! He was cooking up some corn and tofu. Ricky said, "Tofu tastes like chicken!" I told him, "Pork chops taste like chicken! And if you don't get me some meat, I'm gonna put your ass on the grill." That was the last time I was invited to a veggie barbecue.

Even though I am against vegetarian barbecues, I have to give your man props for trying to take care of his health. That's a good thing! The healthier he is, the better the sex. I understand you'd be mad if you reunited with your man and he said, "Guess what? I've had a change in my career plans. I'm a big-time drug dealer now. I'm going to be bagging my product on the kitchen table on Wednesday nights, so you're going to have to reschedule your book club." But your boyfriend hasn't become a criminal; he's trying to better himself. Instead of wishing he would go back in time, maybe you should grab a yoga mat and get to stretching. And from what I hear, perfecting your downward-facing dog can improve your downward-facing doggie-style.

# "You've changed! Now please change back."

## LONI LOVE'S GUIDE TO LEAVING WELL ENOUGH ALONE

| Acceptable changes | Unacceptable changes |
| --- | --- |
| He starts working out. | He compares you to his sexy workout partner. |
| He starts going to church. | He starts going to Bible study every night until midnight. |
| He stops drinking. | He starts doing drugs. |
| He stops doing drugs. | He starts drinking again. |
| He starts taking a college course. | The course is "The Joy of Nude Painting." |
| He starts working overtime. | He gets a job at LeRoy's Massage Parlor & Chicken Shack, where you can "release your stress while eatin' the best!" |

*Dear Loni,*

*When my boyfriend and I were breaking up, I complained to all my girlfriends about him. Now we're back together. Of course, my girlfriends still think of him as the jerk I described when we were breaking up. What can I do to get them to give him another chance?*

*Signed,*
*Me and My Big Mouth*

Dear Big Mouth,

Some women love hearing about what's wrong with somebody else's guy. It makes them feel better about whatever is wrong with *their* man. And if they don't have a man, it makes them feel better about that. I'm guessing that to your friends, hearing you talk crap about your boyfriend feels like hearing good news. And what do people do when they hear good news? They tell everybody!

I remember one time when I was mad at Roscoe, I told all my friends that he has a small penis (this is before I enacted my No Talking About His Tiny Penis policy). My exact words were, "Roscoe's dick is as small as a toothpick. I should dump his ass." Only we didn't break up. Instead, we made up the very next day. About a week later Roscoe and I went over to my friend Caroline's house for a barbecue. Caroline had a few too many margaritas and started throwing toothpicks at Roscoe from across the room, laughing like a hyena and saying, "If the penis don't fit, you must acquit!" That was the last time I ever complained about my man to my friends.

Eventually, your friends may come around to give your man another chance. In the meantime, keep him as far away from your girls as possible. Years later, Caroline and I crack up anytime we see a toothpick.

*Dear Loni,*

*I made a horrible mistake. What's the best way to apologize to a man?*

*Signed,*
*Full of Remorse*

Dear Remorse,

I think apologies should fit the crime. So if your man is angry because you ate the last piece of pecan pie, then you should bake (or, in my case, buy) him another dessert. If you slept with his brother, you should offer him your sister. If you don't have a sister, a friend will do.

My friend Emma once had to pull out all the stops to make the perfect apology. Emma is a very suspicious woman. Too suspicious, it turns out. She had been dating Raymond for three years and even though he gave her no reason to worry, she was convinced he was cheating on her. One day she decided to follow his car and watched as Raymond met an attractive woman on the stoop of a big house. Raymond and the woman walked inside and Emma went crazy. She took her wood-handled umbrella out of the backseat of her car, marched up to the house, and started smashing the windows, like she was about to rob somebody. Hearing the sound of shattering glass, Raymond and his companion ran out of the house. The woman was hysterical, and it turns out she was also a real estate agent. Raymond had been looking to buy the house before he asked Emma to marry him.

To apologize, Emma paid the down payment on the house, repaired the windows, and paid for therapy for the real estate agent. Emma's apology worked because it was crime-appropriate, and that's always more meaningful than a "please forgive me" blow job. Although, if you really messed up you might want to throw in a blow job to sweeten the deal. Like my friend Lisa the exotic-dancer-turned-lawyer always says, there's almost nothing a good blow job won't fix.

*Dear Loni,*

*I got drunk at my husband's family reunion and flirted with his brother. It meant nothing, but the next day my husband packed up his stuff and moved out. How do I get him to take me back?*

*Signed,*
*In a Mess*

Dear Mess,

This is the very reason I believe everyone should have a two-drink limit at family reunions. Someone is always flirting with someone else's husband and causing a fight. But if your husband moved out, I'm guessing this isn't the first time you've flirted with someone in front of him.

If I were you, I would take this time to do some soul-searching about your priorities. If you want to keep your marriage together, you're going to have to focus on your relationship and stop flirting with other men. That means no more going to the butcher shop dressed in hot pants and asking for a giant sausage, no more shopping in the hardware store sucking on a lollipop and asking for a handyman to lay some pipe, and no more answering the door for the pizza deliveryman dressed in a robe that just happens to fall open as you count out his tip.

If you want your man, respect your man. If you want his brother, well, that's a different problem.

> "I don't know why you're so mad.
> It's not like I hit your mother.
> I just tapped her."

## LONI LOVE'S GUIDE TO THINGS
## HE WILL NEVER GET OVER

- You sleep with another man.
- You sleep with a woman without him.
- You full-body tackle him in touch football.
- You tell him you like that new position he tried because your ex used to do it all the time.
- You put his original, signed Joe Montana jersey in the washer and dryer because it "smelled funny."
- You beat him at *Call of Duty*.
- You deadlift more weight than he does.
- You tell him his momma smells like mothballs.

# 6

# CHEATING

*ttention, women of the* world! I know plenty of you lie awake at night, missing valuable beauty sleep, wondering if your man is dipping his tea bag in another woman's cup. Well, I'm here to let you know that not all men have wandering eyes (or hands, or penises). Faithful men—and there are plenty of them out there—behave differently than cheating men. The problem is so many women have been trained to be on the lookout for cheaters that they don't know what to look for in a man who will keep his ass at home. Ladies, before you start hacking his e-mail and checking his pockets, save yourself some time by reviewing Loni Love's Signs of a Faithful Man.

First of all, observe the way your man uses the phone. Cheaters are sneaky and their cell phones are the hub of their covert activities. This is where they weave their web of deceit, making illicit plans and scheduling clandestine rendezvous. That's why a cheater will always keep as much distance as possible between his woman and his phone.

Have you ever had a man come flying out of the bathroom with his pants around his ankles because he hears his cell phone ringing? That guy's a cheater. In fact, any man who does a shoulder roll to keep you from answering his phone is not to be trusted.

On the other hand, a man who gives you complete access to his cell has nothing to hide. If it rings and he asks you to answer because he's busy doing a crossword puzzle, that's your man. If he wants you to look through his contacts for Aunt Betty's number, you're all good. If he asks you to check his phone's calendar for the day the two of you first met and he marked the date with smiley-face emoticons, you've got a keeper (or else you're dating a thirteen-year-old girl). If you're in a serious relationship, you should be able to answer your man's phone without his having a heart attack, even if it rings in the middle of the night.

You also want to consider how secretive your man is about his computer use. Cheaters do all kinds of things they're not supposed to do online, like post profiles on dating websites or send naked pictures to cougars. That's why a cheater will clear his search history or close the laptop the minute you walk into the room.

A faithful man's computer is like an open book for you to read any time you like. Not only will he leave his Facebook page open (feel free to delete those unflattering pictures he took of you at his brother's wedding), he'll never clear his computer's browser history. Of course, this means you'll be able to check out all his searches, some of which may alarm you, like "his and hers Star Trek Halloween costumes," "cutest pictures of kittens ever!" or "break dancing for beginners." Your faithful man might even give you his computer password. If it's the anniversary of your first kiss you have nothing to worry about.

Faithful men are also very good about involving you in their lives—whether you like it or not. You'll be invited to every family get-together, every work function, and every night out with his friends from college.

Your faithful man will tell you all about the personal problems of his closest pals (yes, men do gossip), and if he has female friends they'll know who you are and call to tell you what to get him for his birthday. When you're out together, your faithful guy will introduce you as his girl, his girlfriend, his woman, his lady love, or, if he's into sports, his MVP. Of course this also means he's likely to grab your ass in public, kiss you in church, and fondle your breasts at his grandmother's wake, because if he's not getting it anywhere else, he's going to want it from you, all the time.

The thing faithful men are *not* very good at is mystery. But that's a good thing. A little mystery is great for summer flings or affairs with guys with foreign accents, but not for real relationships. A faithful man never leaves you wondering what he's up to and he never makes you feel like he's keeping you a secret. He may not be as exciting as the guy you hooked up with behind the banquet hall during your high school reunion, but when it comes to a serious relationship, a faithful guy is a girl's best friend.

> ## "I cheated on my husband and it was the best sex I ever had. Do you think I can get the other guy to give my husband some pointers?"
>
> (Everything you need to know about his wandering eye, your lustful heart, and the things that really go down in the Boom Boom Room.)

Dear Loni,

My boyfriend cheated on me. I want us to work things out, but I don't know if I can trust him. How can I make this relationship work?

Signed,
Concerned

Dear Concerned,

I remember the time my then boyfriend, William, admitted he slept with Candy Bush, a dancer from the local gentlemen's club. I forgave him but couldn't let go of the thought of William having sex with someone else. I kept thinking, *What does she have that I don't?* I was so obsessed. I decided to surprise William with a stripper pole in the bedroom. I figured, if sexy dancing is what he likes, I'll give it a try. I told William to call me Sweet Cheeks, strapped on some five-inch Lucite heels, grabbed the pole, and started doing the Tootsie Roll. Well, no one told me the pole had a weight limit. I tried to swing on it and ended up flying across the room and landing with a stiletto in my butt. When Sweet Cheeks became Bruised Cheeks, I realized no good was going to come from my trying to compete with William's one-night stand. If I was willing to take him back, I had to leave the past behind us.

It's normal in a situation like this to have trouble trusting your man. Instead, focus on trusting your own intuition and have faith that if something is going on, you'll figure it out. As Momma Love always says, what's done in the dark will eventually come to light, meaning sooner or later a cheating man will get caught. Especially if his woman is in touch with her intuition. In the meantime, if you want to give this relationship another try, you're going to have to do what I did with William and put your man's cheating behind you. Just leave the pole to the professionals.

*Dear Loni,*

*I'm dating a professional athlete. We met at a club. My girl-friends say I am crazy because all athletes are cheaters. Is this true?*

*Signed,*
*Worried*

Dear Worried,

You should be worried. And not because your man is an athlete, but because he's a man. For a lot of men, cheating is a crime of opportunity, meaning in most cases if you give a man the opportunity, sooner or later he'll come home with glitter on his collar, smelling like regret.

Now think about the life of an athlete: he's rich, famous, and on the road. Plus, the kind of women who flock to a sports star often aren't wearing panties. If you were to create the perfect opportunity to cheat, it would be the life of an athlete . . . or a touring stand-up comic.

Touring comics travel to different cities every week and perform for thousands of people. After a show, it's not unusual for a comic to come to the front of the club for a meet-and-greet with the audience. You'd be surprised by how available the women make themselves, especially once they've put back a few drinks. I've seen ladies of all ages and persuasions pull out a breast for a comic to sign, drop their pants to show off an ass tattoo, or slip a comic their cell number with an X-rated note promising all kinds of sexual acts. And this is just what the fans do with me.

Of course, some men never cheat. It's just not in their nature. But for most men, staying faithful is a matter of mind over penis. You need to be on his mind, so she can't get to his penis. How do you do this? By making your connection as strong as possible. Spend quality time together; make your relationship about more than just sex. Become best friends, because men are less likely to cheat on their BFFs. But remember, if you're dating an athlete (or a comic), he'll be facing plenty of temptation. And Momma Love always says, if your man likes cherry pie, do you really want him working the overnight shift at Wanda's all-night pie factory? Good luck, girl!

"Are you sure those panties in your glove compartment belong to your mother? Because she doesn't look like a woman who wears animal prints."

### LONI LOVE'S SIGNS
### YOUR MAN IS CHEATING (AGAIN)

- He comes home without his underwear and says he got robbed.
- He tells you he wants to be a good son so he plans on visiting his mom every Saturday night, until three in the morning.
- You tell him you have to go away for the weekend, and he starts packing your bag.
- He has a business trip come up unexpectedly ... but he works at Jiffy Lube.
- You ask him why he smells like Astroglide, and he says he got sprayed by a tester at the drugstore.

*Dear Loni,*

*My man flirts with women all the time: waitresses, sales clerks, even our daughter's second-grade teacher. He says it's harmless fun, but I'm not sure. What do you think?*

*Signed,*
*Wondering*

Dear Wondering,

Sometimes what looks like innocent flirting is really a cover-up for something much more serious.

My friend Holland had a husband we called Flirty Frank. He would peer over his sunglasses, which he wore even at night; slowly look a woman up and down, lingering on the area between her neck and her knees; and then say, "You have beautiful eyes." I found Frank's flirting a little suspect, but Holland would always have an explanation. She'd say, "He likes attention," or "He's just being friendly," or "Open-mouth kissing is part of his culture." One day, Holland called me very upset. Frank had gone over to lend their neighbor a hose to water her lawn. But when Holland went into her garage, she discovered the hose coiled by the back door. Assuming Frank had forgotten it, she hoisted it over her shoulder and went over to the neighbor's house. To her surprise, she found Frank watering the neighbor's bush with his own damn hose!

Holland finally had to admit she had been making excuses for her husband and his "affectionate" ways. As a wife or girlfriend, you have a right to check your man's behavior. So grab your red Sharpie and get to checking! If you can't find a marker, ask the second-grade teacher to lend you hers.

# "No, squeezing the neighbor's ass is not just another way of saying hello."

## LONI LOVE'S GUIDE TO MEN'S BEHAVIOR

| Innocent flirting | Flirting that might lead to foreplay | Straight-up sexual harassment |
| --- | --- | --- |
| Telling your mom she is still a spring chicken | Telling your mom she is a sexy chicken | Telling your mom he wants to see her chicken |
| Telling your nanny he can't live without her | Telling your nanny he wants to live with her | Telling your nanny if she becomes a live-in, he'll move you out |
| Telling a waitress she has a pretty smile | Telling a waitress he would like to see more of her pretty smile | Telling a waitress he can do things that will wipe the smile right off her face |
| Telling the music teacher she has a nice voice | Telling the music teacher she's singing his tune | Telling the music teacher he can make her hit notes she's never sung before |

*Dear Loni,*

*I have been dating a married guy for some time. I know it's wrong, but he insists he's only staying in the marriage because his wife is emotionally unbalanced. Well, I just found out he's been having an affair with his assistant as well. I feel so betrayed. I'm wondering if I should tell his wife.*

*Signed,*
*Hurt Mistress*

Dear Hurt,

So you want to call up his "unbalanced" wife to tell her, "Your husband is cheating on us"? Get the fuck outta here.

Seriously, what are you trying to accomplish? Revenge against your cheating man? All he has done is stay true to himself. This is how he gets down, and you should have known that from the cheating relationship he was having with you. If he is the chronic cheater he appears to be, his wife probably already knows. If she doesn't know, it's not your job to tell her. It's the job of the wife's best friend, sister, or hairdresser, whom her husband is probably also banging.

Cheaters cheat and if you get with a cheater, sooner or later he's going to cheat on you. Instead of telling his wife and causing her all sorts of stress, why don't you invest your energy in getting out of this relationship and finding a man who isn't already taken?

*Dear Loni,*

*I've been dating a man for about a year now who's in a relationship with another woman. In the beginning, I didn't mind being the girl on the side. It was just casual sex. But lately I've developed feelings. Should I stick around and hope he'll break up with his girlfriend, or should I get out now?*

> *Signed,*
> *Want to Be More Than a Side Piece*

Dear Side Piece,

This is the very reason I don't recommend women get into sexual relationships with men who are already involved. If you have casual sex, or what I like to call "casualty sex," with another woman's man, sooner or later someone will get hurt.

So let's keep it real: it's unlikely that he's going to break up with his girlfriend and make you his one and only. But for argument's sake, let's say you're the exception, and he dumps his girl and the two of you become an item. Chances are he'll eventually find a new side piece and then you'll be the one getting cheated on. Why? Because you're dealing with the type of man I call The Ringmaster.

My cousin Dinky is a Ringmaster. He's very handsome and charismatic and always has at least three relationships going at once. His love life is a circus. One day, Dinky broke it down for me. He says his main woman, whom he calls "Wifey," is the one who has his heart. Dinky says the problem with Wifey is that her favorite sex position is missionary, she doesn't like playing video games, and her baby toenail is missing. Of course, these aren't real problems, they're simply excuses Dinky gives to justify his circus.

Dinky says his number two girl is there for "backup." She does crazy acrobatics in bed, and is really good at Xbox. "Wifey and number two are a perfect set," says Dinky. "I can't have one without the other." Then there's the out-of-town chick. When things get too stressful at home, Dinky runs away "on business," or as I like to say, to clown around.

Dinky is my cousin, but I don't agree with his lifestyle choices. I've had to listen to too many women calling me in tears, complaining about being part of Dinky's sideshow. It sounds to me like the man whom you are patiently waiting for is not boyfriend material. He is heartbreak material, just like Dinky. Don't let yourself be part of this man's circus. You deserve to be a star. Now make like Meryl Streep and get to shining!

> "It's okay if I spend Christmas, my birthday, and our anniversary alone. I already had plans to watch Lifetime and weep into a gallon tub of Ben and Jerry's anyway."

## LONI LOVE'S TOP FIVE REASONS NOT TO BE THE GIRL ON THE SIDE

- You will never be able to change your Facebook status from "It's complicated."
- You'll have to give an Oscar-worthy performance when he introduces you to his wife.
- You may have to hear the words "You're getting an abortion, right?"
- The only relative he will introduce you to is his weird cousin J-Dog who lives in an abandoned shed.
- In public, he'll introduce you as his cousin J-Dog's "special friend."

*Dear Loni,*

*Sometimes my husband goes out with the guys. He's always told me that they're having a few beers at a sports bar. Recently his best friend let it slip that my husband is a frequent client of the Boom Boom Room at the back of a seedy strip club. My husband says I have nothing to worry about and that he's not doing anything wrong. What do you think?*

*Signed,*
*Keep Your Hands off My*
*Husband*

Dear Hands,

First of all, if your husband tells you nothing is going on in the Boom Boom Room, he is lying. My cousin Dinky is a big fan of Boom Boom Rooms. He says the rubbing and tugging that goes on in the back of a strip club would make any wife's head explode. That's why they call it Boom freakin' Boom.

But if you ask me, having Candy Bush rub on your man is only part of the problem. The bigger issue is that your man isn't telling you the truth about how he spends his time. What else might he be lying to you about? Maybe all those times he told you that you looked great in a dress, he really thought you looked like the Pillsbury Doughboy. Or maybe he tells you he trusts your advice, when really he gets his guidance from a Magic 8 Ball. Or maybe when he told you he got a promotion to manager, he actually meant a demotion, and now he's working in the mailroom, insisting everyone call him "boss."

Sometimes, when a truth comes to light it's the universe's way of telling you to take a closer look at what's really going on. Honey, your man has been deceiving you. My boo Dr. Drew would be proud of what I'm about to say: take this opportunity to seek some counseling for yourself and your husband so he can stop the lying and you can regain the trust.

*Dear Loni,*

*My friend posted an Instagram picture of herself with her new man enjoying a romantic weekend in Paris. The problem is, her new man is the same man my other good friend just started dating. These women don't know each other, but I am friends with both of them. What should I do?*

*Signed,*
*Stuck in the Middle*

Dear Stuck,

Men are so sloppy. You'd think Loverboy would have enough sense to cover his damn face when he was being photographed while on a romantic excursion. But he didn't, and now here you are, knowing way too much about his weekend activities. If these women were only casual friends of yours, I might tell you to keep your mouth shut and let the stilettos fall where they may. But since these are your real friends, you have a duty to pass on the information that can save both of them a lot of wasted time.

I remember once being in a similar situation with my friend Dawn. Dawn was my best friend at college. One night she and I went on a double date with our boyfriends Cheney and Roland. During dinner, my boyfriend, Cheney, left early announcing he had to go to work. Well, it turns out that Cheney had told Roland that he had another date later that night. He was double dipping! Roland told Dawn, and Dawn, not wanting to stir things up, chose not to tell me. Later she defended her actions by saying, "I knew you would find out sooner or later." She was right. Eventually I did find out, but not before I had spent months dating a man who wasn't worth my time. I told Dawn that she had let me down as a friend. This is a woman I would have shared my last piece of bacon with, and she didn't even see fit to share this vital information. Best friends don't let best friends date idiots.

Dawn should have told me about the date so I could stalk Cheney, see this other girl had nothing on me, and walk away with my pride intact. This is the American way. My friend was a traitor.

*Dear Loni,*

*I went away on vacation and cheated on my husband with this totally sexy man I met on the beach. It was the best sex I ever had. Do I need to confess?*

*Signed,*
*Sexy on the Beach*

Dear Sexy,

Sounds like someone had one too many mai tais! Now, I'm not a big fan of cheating. I believe if you really love your partner, you owe it to that person not to do things that can break his (or her) heart. Still, I know sometimes people get carried away, especially on vacation. You might meet a beautiful man who looks *just* like your husband did twenty years and fifty pounds ago, you might accidentally get drunk, and your bathing suit might accidentally fall off. The next thing you know, the two of you are accidentally having sex. Shit happens.

But if you're going to cheat (against my recommendation!), it's important you do as little damage as possible: don't bring home any diseases, make any new babies, or get involved with a crazy person who thinks the two of you are in love. As long as you use protection, a one-night stand in a foreign country, with a man who doesn't know where you live, is the least risky cheating there is. Once it's over, it's over. There is no messy aftermath and you can walk away with only your memories.

As far as confessing goes, who's going to benefit from your spilling the beans? I think sometimes people tell themselves they are confessing to be "honest," when really it's because they can't live with the guilt. But guilt is the price you are going to have to pay for your fun in the sun. If you tell your man some dude on the beach turned you into a sexual dynamo, it's only going to break his heart.

My advice? Keep your mouth shut. And if you're feeling really guilty, make it up to your man by showing him an extra-good time in bed. Just make sure that in the heat of passion you don't give yourself away by screaming, "I learned this position on vacation!"

> ## "If you're gonna cheat,
> ## you have to follow the rules."

### LONI LOVE'S TIPS FOR
### A CHEATING HEART

- Don't cuddle after sex; it only encourages intimacy. But do let him rub your feet.
- Keep your cell phone under the pillow, next to your gun.
- Always use a condom and, if he seems like a real player, a full-body hazmat suit.
- Never use your real name. Instead, introduce yourself as Sexy Susie from Scandinavia. That way if he ever tries to Google you, he'll get distracted by a porn site about Nordic women.
- Don't brag to your friends about your sexcapades; each one of them should be considered a potential security leak. If you need to share the details, give yourself a pseudonym, write a book called *Eleven Shades of Orange*, and become a bestselling author of erotic fiction.
- Sit back and ask yourself, "What will happen if I get caught?" If you're not willing to live with the consequences, don't cheat at all.

*Dear Loni,*

*My boyfriend has suddenly started doing all kinds of new things in bed. Some of them are kind of kinky. Do you think he's cheating, and learning all these moves from the other woman? I have a feeling something's going on.*

*Signed,*
*Suspicious*

Dear Suspicious,

Hell yeah, he might be cheating! Or he could be watching a lot of porn. Or he might be reading sex manuals. The point is, there are a lot of different reasons a man might suddenly step it up in the bedroom. But if you feel he's cheating, you need to investigate. Ask him what's up with the moves. If he gives you a story that sounds suspicious, like "These new positions came to me in a dream," look him square in the eye and ask if he's cheating. If he says no and you still don't believe him, do some detective work. In the days of HIV, it's a woman's right to do whatever is necessary to learn the true sexual habits of her partner. Check his pockets, his phone bill, and his drawers for evidence like condom wrappers, phone numbers, love notes, and ladies' panties. But you should be prepared for what you may find.

When my friend Alice started dating her new boyfriend

Jayson, she thought it would be a good idea to do what she calls a "background check," which is basically her snooping through his things when he's taking a shower. One night when Jayson was cleaning up after getting home from the gym, Alice jumped on his computer to search his browsing history. She was shocked to find Jayson was spending a lot of time researching Furries. Furries are people who get turned on by dressing up like big furry stuffed animals. Alice told me this over lunch one day; she said, "That explains the panda-bear suit for my birthday." I tried to console Alice, but I couldn't stop picturing Jayson dressed as a big-ass koala bear, with a hard-on.

Sex is full of mystery. People get turned on by all kinds of things. Your man might be learning new moves because he's cheating, or he might finally be comfortable enough with you to let his true freakish self shine through. Either way, you need to know the truth.

> ## "I snooped on my man and I found a jar of spicy pickles and a pair of handcuffs in his underwear drawer."

### LONI LOVE'S GUIDE TO
### THE DOWNSIDE OF SNOOPING

| What you're looking for | What you might find instead |
| --- | --- |
| Nude pictures | Pictures of kids you didn't know he had |
| Love notes | Divorce papers addressed to you |
| Sexy e-mails | E-mails from his parole officer |
| Voice mails from other women | Voice mails from the STD clinic telling him to come in ASAP |
| Lipstick stains on his clothes | Ladies' clothes, in his size |
| Dirty text messages from Janet | Dirty text messages from Jake |

*Dear Loni,*

*My husband cheated on me with one of our neighbors. I've de-cided to forgive him, but I'm still angry with our neighbor. Since I found out, I've been leaving dog poop on her front stoop and hiding in the bushes to watch her step in it when she rushes out the door to go to work. I know it's childish, but I can't stop. I am so ANGRY. What should I do?*

*Signed,*
*Full of Rage*

Dear Rage,

You know what I think? I think you're still angry at your husband, who betrayed you, but it's difficult to be angry at someone you live with, so instead you are projecting all your rage onto your neighbor.

All my life, I've been helping my girlfriends solve their relationship problems. I can't tell you how many times I've seen women fall into this pattern. I call it Blame the One You *Don't* Live With syndrome. Don't get me wrong; your neighbor broke the code: you're not supposed to sleep with another woman's man. But your husband is wrong too. In fact, what he did was worse. He cheated with a neighbor and now you can't even go to the annual block party without wondering if everyone knows.

My friend Rosemary was really upset when she found out

her hubby of twelve years had an affair with a woman he met at a conference. Her husband apologized profusely, and she took him back quicker than you can cook bacon in a microwave.

Rosemary reconciled with him for the sake of her children, but she couldn't stop thinking about the other woman. She found out her name, Googled her, checked her Facebook updates, and eventually started calling her at the office. The woman finally called the cops and reported Rosemary as a stalker. That was Rosemary's wake-up call. She started seeing a therapist and realized that her obsession was really just her way of dealing with the anger she had toward her husband.

Once Rosemary was finally able to tell her husband how she felt, she stopped worrying about the other woman and started focusing on her court-mandated five hundred hours of community service.

*Dear Loni,*

*For the past few months my husband has been very distant. I know it's wrong, but one night I went on his computer and snooped through his e-mails. It turns out my husband has been in touch with a girl he used to know in high school. There's nothing sexual about the e-mails, but the two of them are obviously very close. I'm so confused. What should I do?*

*Signed,*
*Lonely in My Own Home*

Dear Lonely,

Your husband is having what experts, like my boo Dr. Drew, call an emotional affair. He is involved in an intimate relationship with another woman and you have every right to feel confused.

One time I was dating a man named Denzel. Yep, I found me a man named Denzel! One of the things that made Denzel so perfect for me is we both shared a love of going out for dinner and trying new cuisines. At night, Denzel and I would lie in bed and talk about an idea we called "around the world one menu at a time." Our plan was to go on a world tour by eating at exotic restaurants right there in our city.

One night, I was over at Denzel's apartment when he went out for some wine, leaving me alone in his living room. I was minding my business, when I just *happened* to open a drawer because I was looking for a pen. (That's my story and I'm sticking to it!) While digging around, I found a stack of menus from some of the best restaurants in the city. There were Thai, Indian, and Hungarian menus. He even had one from a raw-food, macrobiotic vegetarian spot, which I assumed Denzel had included as some kind of joke.

I was so touched that Denzel was going to all this trouble to start planning our whirlwind culinary tour. I went home the next day with a big smile on my face. A few days went by without Denzel's mentioning our tour. The days turned to weeks and still no mention of our eating out. In fact, just the opposite. Whenever I suggested we go out for dinner, Denzel would say he didn't feel like it and suggest that we just chill at home. I can't tell you how many nights we ended up sitting in front of the TV eating Hot Pockets. Finally, I couldn't take it anymore. I said, "Denzel, the other day I came across a stack of fancy menus. When are we going on our world tour?" Denzel got a strange look on his face. Finally, he broke down and told me the truth. A woman he worked with had started a food blog and the two of them had been going out every lunch hour for lavish meals, which she paid for. What the hell? All these restaurants I was looking forward to eating at, Denzel was experiencing with another woman! I was hurt, angry, and hungry. After treating myself to a continental breakfast, an English high tea, and a Spanish siesta, I broke it off with Denzel: one, for eating out behind my back, and two, for being a cheapskate and using his friend to eat for free.

The fact is, it's never okay for a man to have a close friendship with a woman that involves secrets and lies. So you have two options: you can lay your cards on the table and tell your man you snooped, and the two of you can get to work rebuilding your relationship. Or you can keep the snooping to yourself while you focus on developing a deeper bond with your husband. Set aside time for the two of you to be alone, with no kids, no cell phones, and no TV to distract you. Ask him how he's feeling about his work, your family, the marriage. Share your feelings too. Obviously, an emotional connection is what he wants. With a little effort you can make it happen.

> "I said, 'Let's talk about our feelings,'
> not 'Let's feel each other up.'"

## LONI LOVE'S FIVE BEST WAYS TO CONNECT WITH YOUR MAN (WITHOUT HAVING SEX)

- Go to an all-you-can-eat buffet and see who taps out first.
- Think of fun questions to get to know each other better, such as, "Do you have any children I don't know about?"
- Curl up in your pajamas and watch an hour of Lifetime and an hour of ESPN, and then spend the rest of the night explaining what was so damn important about the show you just made the other person watch.
- Take him to Armani to try on suits and tell him how handsome he looks, then go to Men's Wearhouse and buy him a knockoff.
- Make homemade sushi and eat it off each other. If your man doesn't like sushi, you can just lay some cold cuts on your back, hand him a jar of mustard, and tell him to go to town.

# 7

# FRIENDS AND FAMILY

*A lot of my friends* swear by the rule "You can predict how well a man will treat you by looking at how he treats his mother." I think you can get an even better idea of how he'll treat you if you look at his relationships with his whole family, including the dog. Believe me, if he comes home and his dog runs into the other room, there's definitely something wrong with your man.

There are two kinds of men you need to look out for. The first is the guy who has *no* relationship with his family at all. Now, I'm not talking about the man who lost both his parents in a tragic car accident. I'm talking about the guy who has deep and unresolved issues with his parents that have left him so bitter that he refuses to have anything to do with them. This is the guy who's still pissed that his parents didn't support his dreams of becoming a glass blower, or wouldn't let him move back into their house and set up a pizza oven in the basement, or "abandoned" him when they retired to Florida the year he turned thirty-seven. You don't want to get into a relationship with a guy who's been giving his parents the silent treatment since college, because that would be like dating a teenager trapped in a grown man's body (I prefer a grown man trapped in the body of a twenty-one-year-old running back for the New England Patriots). A man who thinks an appropriate response to conflict is feeling sorry for himself is not a man capable of having an adult relationship. He'd be better off playing a sad-faced rodeo clown at the county fair.

You also need to be very careful about getting involved with a man who's *too* close to his family. Specifically, you should avoid any man who's the little prince in a family full of females. This man can do no wrong in the eyes of his mother, sisters, aunts, and cousins and seeks their advice every time he has a problem. This guy will also have an annoying habit of working his mother's, sister's, or cousin's "expert" opinion into the conversation, as though he's quoting Oprah. Just imagine, you're trying to talk to your man about his life goals and he pipes up with, "Well, my sister says lying on the sofa eating Cheetos is part of my creative process."

You also want to stay away from a guy who always takes the side of his family members over you during an argument. This is the same guy who'll expect you to lend him bail money to get his little brother out of jail or invite his out-of-town cousins to stay at your house like you're running a Holiday Inn. It's fine for a man to look out for his relatives, but in a serious relationship *you* should come first. Of course, I'm not saying he needs to automatically take your side in an argument either. A smart man knows that when women start to bicker, his job is to quietly step into the other room and only intervene if he hears breaking glass or someone asking where he keeps his handgun.

Now, sometimes the problem isn't how the man treats his relatives, it's how his relatives treat you. A classic scenario is the mother who's still in love with her son's ex. This woman will have a family get-together and invite her son and his ex but not you. Remember, his mother may be old and set in her ways. She and your man's ex may have had a beautiful relationship, and his mother might not have wanted it to end. Give her a few months to adjust. But if you ever catch her watching as you wipe down the kitchen counter, shaking her head sadly, and saying, "Marcia never did it that way," you're in trouble. This roughly translates into "Get out of my son's life, you tramp. I want Marcia back." In that case, you only have one option: smile sweetly and tell his mother that the next time your man's crazy cousins come to visit, they can stay at Marcia's place.

# "Is your uncle having a seizure? Because he told me he's grabbing my ass to keep from falling."

(Everything you need to know about his doting mother, his gossiping friends, and his uncle with the wandering hands.)

Dear Loni,

My man is smart and ambitious, but his friends, who he's known since high school, are a bunch of immature slackers who only want to drink beer and play video games. My boyfriend turns into a total idiot when he is with them. How do I get my man to break up with his friends?

Signed,
Love the Man, Hate His
Crew

Dear Crew,

Girl, there are certain things in the world that will remain a mystery: UFOs, the Egyptian pyramids, and a man's choice of friends.

While you might not like them, your boyfriend's friends are guys he has a history with. Whatever you do, you can't ask him to choose between you and his crew. That would be like asking him to choose between an ice-cold beer and a crispy Hot Pocket; it's a choice no man should have to make.

Instead of trying to get him to quit his friends, why don't you designate certain nights (say, every other Friday) as Fun with Friends Night. On those evenings, your man gets to spend time with his knuckleheaded friends while you do something fun for you. Start a book club, or, if you're like the women in my family, start a drinking club. Invite your girls over and each of you take a turn making a different cocktail. Just stay away from that 100-proof rum. It took me two days to clean up after Momma Love invited her friends over for "Bible study."

> "My idea of an 'awesome night' does not include your best friend falling asleep naked on our front lawn."

## LONI LOVE'S GUIDE TO HIS FRIENDS' UNACCEPTABLE BEHAVIOR

| Acceptable | Not acceptable |
| --- | --- |
| Gets drunk and passes out at your place | Gets drunk and makes a pass at you |
| Hosts a weekly poker night | Hosts a weekly strip-poker night |
| Invites you and your man on a double date | Invites you and your man to switch dates |
| Watches the game at your house | Watches *every* game at your house |
| Plays touch football at the family barbecue | Scratches his balls at the family barbecue |

*Dear Loni,*

*My boyfriend lives in his mother's basement. Once in a while I spend the night. The last time I was over there we had a few drinks and things got a little crazy. Just as I was hanging upside down off the edge of the bed, I opened my eyes and saw my boyfriend's mother standing at the door with a basket of his folded laundry. I am mortified. How can I ever show my face in that house again?*

*Signed,*
*Caught in the Act*

Dear Caught,

Oh, girl, these are tough times and I know a lot of grown men have had to move back home with their mommas. But while you're worried about his momma catching you getting your freak on, what you *should* be worried about is why a grown man has his momma doing his laundry! After what I've been through, my vajayjay immediately dries up when I hear about a man who can't take care of himself.

My ex Max was a forty-year-old advertising executive who owned his own home, and yet his mother pampered him like he was a little boy. One day I went over to Max's place and there was his mother, in an apron, waxing his car. When she finished, she cooked him dinner, washed and ironed his clothes, did his taxes, gave him a shave, and clipped his toenails. Max is so used to his mother taking care of him, he assumed he would always be waited on hand and foot by a woman. As you can imagine, that didn't sit too well with me.

I'm out every night taking care of my career. I'm not about to come home and take care of a grown-ass man. I think the division of household labor should be fifty-fifty. He can moisturize my exquisite knees and I'll make dinner. And by "make dinner" I mean "order Chinese takeout." I knew the minute Max asked me when his laundry would be washed and ironed that we would never last as a couple. Trust me when I tell you, a grown man who lives in his momma's basement and doesn't do his own laundry is not a keeper. The problem is, some women are so desperate for a relationship they'll make all kinds of excuses, like "He's self-employed," or "They are a very tight-knit family," or "He's gonna put that rent money he's saving toward a diamond ring!"

Max and I were finished, but before I had a chance to dump him, his mother showed up at my door saying she'd come over to break up with me. It took everything I had not to tell her to kiss me where the sun don't shine. I respect my elders, so I had Momma Love tell her off instead.

*Dear Loni,*

*I am dating a great guy but his thirteen-year-old daughter hates me. How can I win her over?*

*Signed,*
*Not the Evil Stepmother*

Dear Stepmother,

Honey, don't you know thirteen-year-old girls don't like anything? When I was thirteen, I didn't like boys, green beans, wet grass, Madonna's "Holiday" music video, white bread, wheat bread, sourdough bread, red socks, pickles, and my entire eighth-grade class. And as you can see, I turned out perfectly fine.

In addition to being moody, this young lady may also be feeling some jealousy. Until you came along, she might have been the apple of Daddy's eye. Now Daddy is eyeing something even juicier. It's only natural for his little princess to feel threatened. She's just protecting her territory. Or maybe she's still fantasizing that her parents are going to get back together. In her mind, you might be the only thing standing in their way.

My advice to you is to spend some time trying to get to know this child. Is she a girly girl? A tomboy? A skater chick? A drama geek? Find out what she likes and don't be shy about trying to buy her affection. A trip to the nail salon, a new outfit, or tickets to a show can go a long way in helping smooth over the rough edges in your relationship.

When I was growing up, my mom dated a man I called Mr. Greg. At first I didn't like Mr. Greg because I enjoyed having Mom to myself. Plus, he wore too much Midnight Velveteen cologne. You could smell Mr. Greg coming and going. But Mr. Greg turned out to be a real gentleman. Whenever he took my mother out, he'd always take me along. We went to the movies, restaurants, the park. Mr. Greg treated me like I was important, and that made a big impression on me.

As long as you're consistent, you're patient, and you don't push too hard, your boyfriend's daughter will eventually come around. If not, it's only five years before you can call her a bratty little bitch to her face.

# "Let's go buy a puppy!"

## LONI LOVE'S KEY PHRASES FOR WINNING OVER HIS KIDS

- "You know what this breakfast needs? More candy!"
- "I agree. Your dad *is* a poopy head."
- "No school today. You have a hangnail. You need to rest."
- "Your teacher's an idiot. Your paper comparing Lil Wayne to Mahatma Gandhi is genius."
- "I found your father's credit card. Let's go to the mall!"
- "You need a bigger allowance."
- "Your father's out of town this weekend. Why don't you invite the entire senior class over for a little get-together?"

*Dear Loni,*

*I'm a single mother and I'm very careful to not bring men around my six-year-old son unless it's serious. Well, I've been dating a wonderful man for six months and I decided it's time to introduce him to my son. It turns out my son HATES him! My sister says I should dump this man right away. She says, "Children are like dogs, they can sense evil." Is this true? Does my son know something I don't?*

*Signed,*
*Mother in Love*

Dear Mother,

I applaud you for being a great single mother; I can tell by your question that your number one priority is your child. Of course, that's not to say you shouldn't have a romantic relationship. You may be a momma, but you ain't dead!

If your child doesn't like your man, you need to find out why. Maybe your son is jealous? If so, help him feel more secure by spending extra time doing activities with him, like flying a kite, shooting marbles, or chasing him around Chuck E. Cheese. And remind your son every day that he is still, and will always be, your number one.

On the other hand, don't rule out the possibility that your new boyfriend said or did something that made your son uncomfortable. It may be inconceivable to you that the man you love could treat your child badly when you're not around, but trust me, it happens all the time. As a comedian I joke a lot, but when it comes to children and dating this is no laughing matter. If you sense something bad is going on, trust your instincts and seek the help of a professional.

Momma Love always says, you can't be too safe. As part of her homeland security plan, she hid surveillance cameras in the light fixtures. Growing up, I thought she had supernatural powers because she always seemed to know if I had given my broccoli to the dog. It was only when I was an adult that I discovered her superpowers didn't come from God, they came from Sony.

*Dear Loni,*

*My fiancé's mother is perfectly nice to me when my fiancé is in the room, but the second he leaves us alone she starts calling me names and saying things like, "It'll be a cold day in hell before I let my son marry a bitch like you." I told my fiancé that his mother has an evil side, but he just laughed it off and said she was making a joke. Loni, this woman is NOT joking. What should I do?*

*Signed,*
*Can't Stand the Bad Vibes*

Dear Can't Stand,

Sounds like you're dealing with a Jekyll-and-Hyde momma! I know because Arnold, my ex live-in boyfriend, had a mother just like that. When I first met Arnold's mother, she would laugh at my jokes, share her recipes, and have meaningful conversations with me. But once Arnold and I decided to move in together, it was a different story. One day, I went to his mother's house to pay her a visit. She answered the door, looked me up and down, and said, "I don't know why my Arnold would move in with you. You're fat and your jokes aren't funny."

Now, I can take a mother making cracks about how I look; as long as her son likes all this sexy, I don't care. But telling me I'm not funny? That means war! I immediately told Arnold what his mother had said. When he confronted her, she told him that I must have misheard her; she was just crazy about me. Yeah, she was crazy all right, and I was about to prove it.

A few nights later, I had Arnold invite his mother over for dinner. Once she arrived, I sent Arnold to the store for some wine. That's when Evil Momma Hyde came out. "You better not make me sick with your cooking," she said. "Look at your fat ass. When I was young, I watched my weight. I was a slim size twelve. And by the way, your weave looks ridiculous." I let her go on and on until Arnold came home. As we sat down to say grace, I pulled out the little digital recorder I had hidden in my bra and hit "play." You should have seen the look on her face!

If you're dealing with a mother who has multiple personalities, your best bet is to ignore her nasty remarks and know that eventually the truth will be revealed. And by that I mean, put a recorder in your bra and catch her in the act.

> ## "I know your mother doesn't like me, but does she have to keep slashing my tires?"

### LONI LOVE'S TIPS FOR GETTING HIS MOTHER TO LIKE YOU

- Go to church with her on Sunday, even when you're hung over.
- Spike her iced tea with Wild Turkey.
- Act like you know nothing about cooking and ask her to show you how it's done.
- Invite her to the ninety-nine-cent store and let her spend fifty dollars.
- Send her over a male stripper named Big Willie Brown.
- Take her to a singles' club and be her wingwoman.
- Stop dating her son.

*Dear Loni,*

*Last weekend my husband and I went to his parents' home for dinner. After dessert, I was in the kitchen cleaning up and my husband's married uncle made a pass at me. He's made comments before, but this is the first time he's become physical. Should I tell my husband or the uncle's wife, or keep the whole thing to myself?*

*Signed,*
*Fondled*

Dear Fondled,

Don't you just hate an uncle who can't keep his hands to himself? One night Roscoe and I had Uncle T-Bone and his wife over for game night, or as we like to call it, "drink night." As we were playing Monopoly, I felt someone put his hand on my knee and rub my thigh. I looked around the table and saw Uncle T-Bone with a big smile on his face, like a fox in a henhouse. I was not having it! Faster than you can say "frozen margaritas," I accidentally-on-purpose knocked the whole pitcher of frosty adult beverage right in his lap. Nothing says "Get your hands off my thigh" like an ice-cold penis.

The next time your husband's uncle grabs your behind, say to him, "Look, Hands McGee, you touch me again and I am going to tell my husband *and* your wife. Then I'm going to tell my cousin Li'l Kill Joy. He just got out of jail and he's not afraid to go back!"

*Dear Loni,*

*I was looking through my boyfriend's photo album and came across a picture of a guy who looked very familiar. When I asked my boyfriend, he said, "That's my douchy brother, Kyle." And then it all came back . . . I had a drunken one-night stand with Kyle after a Green Day concert when I was in college. I know I have to tell my boyfriend because next month he's taking me to his family reunion. What's the best way to break it to him?*

*Signed,*
*My Boyfriend's the Better Brother*

Dear Better Brother,

Did you take any acting classes in high school? Because you are going to need to channel Meryl Streep to pull off what I like to call the "If I say I don't remember, then it's like it didn't happen" maneuver. Here's how it works: go to the reunion with your boyfriend and let him introduce you to his douchy brother. When you meet him, act as though you've never seen him before. If he says he knows you, reply, "You don't look familiar." If he presses the issue, give him a long look, as though you're searching your memory, then slowly nod and say, "Now I remember. You used to work in the mailroom at my old job, right?"

Trust me, no man wants to think that a woman he had sex with forgot all about it. As Momma Love says, the most sensitive part of a man ain't his ding dong, it's his ego.

*Dear Loni,*

*My boyfriend's best friend is a girl he's known since elementary school. I've only met her once and she seemed nice enough, but the other day I found out, through a mutual friend, that she's been bad-mouthing me to my boyfriend. She told him he's a ten and I'm a four and he can do better. What should I do?*

*Signed,*
*I Thought I Was a Seven*

Dear Seven,

Here's what is going on: your boyfriend's "friend" wishes she was more than a friend and she thinks that tearing you down is going to help her chances.

But it's perfectly reasonable for you to expect your man to stand up for you if someone else is insulting you. After my boyfriend Arnold found out about his mother and her Jekyll-and-Hyde ways, he made a point of always stepping up to defend me. One day we were at a family party when his cousin Spoon made a joke about my weight. Arnold didn't miss a beat. He said, "Loni may be a fat-ass, but she's *my* fat-ass." I took that backhanded compliment with pride and told Arnold to shut the hell up.

You need to tell your man it hurt your feelings that someone close to him was talking shit about you. If he acts like this is no big deal, then his friend did you a big favor by giving you an opportunity to see your man's true colors: he's a jerk. In which case she can have him, because *you* deserve better.

## "Your friend said *what?*"

### LONI LOVE'S GUIDE TO HIS SMACK-TALKING FRIENDS

| If she says . . . | You say . . . |
| --- | --- |
| "You're a bitch." | "Thank you!" |
| "I liked his last girlfriend better." | "That's because he was dating your mother." |
| "You might want to put down those cookies." | "You may want to pick up a breath mint." |
| "You'd look better with bigger boobs." | "You'd look better with all your teeth." |
| "You're not his type." | "That's not what he was shouting last night . . . all night!" |

*Dear Loni,*

*My boyfriend's baby momma does not like me. I know this because when she came to pick up her son, she took one look at me and said to my boyfriend, "Keep your nasty ho away from my child." My boyfriend tells me to ignore her. Is there any way to get her to stop being so mean?*

*Signed,*
*Can't We All Just Get Along*

Dear Get Along,

I know just how you feel! My ex Chris has a child with a crazy baby momma who loves drama. This chick would call at all times of the day and night, come by the house unannounced, and insist I leave the room so she and my man could discuss "family business," which consisted of her complaining about me. I realized I had two choices: I could either fight fire with fire and go off on the woman, or I could flip the script and try to turn this grizzly into a teddy bear with a big dose of honey.

Instead of telling his baby momma what I really thought of her, I started complimenting her every chance I had. When I got the urge to tell her, "I'll whoop your ass!" I said, "That's a whoop-ass weave, girl!" Instead of saying, "Don't even think of telling me what to do!" I said, "Girl, how do you do it so well?" And I didn't just tell her nice things to her face. I also utilized the information transportation device known as her child. Every time I was with her son I would say things like, "Did your mother give you that shirt? She has great taste!" Or "Did your mother teach you to do math? She must be a genius!"

Now, you may be asking yourself, "Why would Loni be so nice to a woman who disrespected her?" The reason is this: I know from watching Momma Love raise me and my brother that single mothers are overworked and underappreciated. Sometimes that anger you see is just exhaustion. If you let your boyfriend's baby's mother know you respect her and all she is doing to raise her child, she is sure to warm up to you.

*Dear Loni,*

*My new man has two teenage sons from a previous marriage. They are spoiled-rotten smart-asses who don't clean up after themselves. My man and I are talking about moving in together. What's the best way for me to correct his sons' behavior?*

*Signed,*
*Not the Mom*

Dear Not the Mom,

I once dated a guy named Juan Carlos. J.C. didn't have kids, but he had five sisters and two brothers who had a total of twenty-one children between then. When J.C. would stay at my house for the weekend, his nieces and nephews loved to come by "to say hello." Those kids would treat my home like their own personal clubhouse, eating up all my bacon, using all my toilet paper, and ruining my throw pillows with their sticky little hands. After a few months of this, I decided to itemize everything they used and present Juan Carlos with a bill. It came to $452.62. I haven't seen him or his family since.

   You need to sit down with your man and tell him how you feel about his no-manners-having kiddos. But don't expect them to change. They may be teenagers but they have another decade of growing up to do before they come to their senses. The only thing you can do is make your house less inviting so they'll look for somewhere more fun to hang out, like a Laundromat, an abandoned warehouse, or the parking lot at Bed Bath & Beyond.

# "No, I'm sorry, you can't use the bathroom. Here's a key to the gas station down the street."

## LONI LOVE'S GUIDE TO MAKING A HOUSE *NOT* A HOME

- Keep a lock on the refrigerator.
- Walk around your house singing old Negro spirituals and insisting everybody join in.
- Hand-wash your bras and leave them soaking in the kitchen sink.
- Ask his sons to help you redecorate your place by moving all the furniture around. Then tell them you liked it better the other way. Repeat.
- When you answer the door, burst into tears and say, "I'm so glad you're here; I'm feeling *very* hormonal!"

# 8

# GETTING HITCHED

*I was never the girl* with the scrapbook full of ideas for my fantasy wedding, but I know that for many women marriage is something they dream of all their lives. Marriage can be a beautiful thing if you're committed, devoted, and willing to have a ball and chain tied to your leg until the end of time (I'm such a romantic). But it takes a lot of work. I know because I was once married. And I've hardly told anybody about it until now.

In the spring of 2004, a few months after I decided to leave engineering and pursue my dream of being a comic, I landed a gig performing for the troops in Hawaii. After the show, a fine-ass soldier approached me to say how much he enjoyed my set. He explained he was on leave for the week and asked if I would like to join him for a drink. I was new to the comedy game but I already had a rule not to date any man who tried to pick me up after a show. That's just asking for trouble. He might be a crazy groupie, a broke comedy nerd, or both. But in this case I made an exception. Something felt different about this tall, handsome soldier. He was sweet and sincere and when he looked me in the eye I felt like I had a bellyful of butterflies.

Johnnie and I spent the next four days together, enjoying candlelit dinners and long walks on the beach. We didn't have sex (although you know I was tempted), we just talked and talked, and I had the greatest time in my life. When I returned to Los Angeles, Johnnie and I kept up our romance, spending hours on the phone and seeing each other every chance we had. Johnnie visited me in Los Angeles, and I took trips to Hawaii, where he was stationed. One day, after we'd been seeing each other for almost two years, Johnnie said that for his next leave he wanted us to meet in Las Vegas. I was so excited. I would get to see my honey, hit all the buffets, and catch Cher's fifty-seventh farewell tour!

The drive to Vegas took four hours, and the whole way my heart was pounding in anticipation. But as I pulled up to the address Johnnie had given me, I realized it wasn't a hotel. It was the Clark County courthouse, in downtown Las Vegas. I parked my car, worried about what this might mean. Was Johnnie in trouble? Did I need to call my cousin Skillet for legal advice? I was in such a rush to find him that I almost tripped over Johnnie as I ran up the courthouse steps. He was on bended knee, holding a dozen roses, his hands shaking slightly. "Will you marry me?" he asked, his voice barely above a whisper.

I was so shocked, I blurted out the first thing that came to my mind: "I have to pee!" I darted past Johnnie toward the ladies' room. I had bought two 7-Eleven Big Gulps for the drive, but I also needed a minute to think. This was all so sudden. I wasn't sure about marriage, but I was sure I was in love. I came out of the ladies' room, found my man, and gave him a big hug. "Yes," I said. "Let's do this."

We got a marriage license then headed to a chapel near the

courthouse. During the simple ceremony, I looked over at Johnnie and saw tears in his eyes as the minister said, "You may kiss the bride." And I'll tell you this: as long as I live, I'll probably never have another kiss like the one Johnnie gave me that day. It was the kind of kiss that makes you weak in the knees; it was a true kiss of love. And I was totally sober!

Getting married so suddenly was like living a fairy tale. But soon enough, reality hit. A few months after we were married, Johnnie got assigned to a base in North Carolina and he expected me to move there and join him. By that time my career was really taking off and I knew leaving L.A. was going to bring my career to a halt. We tried to make the relationship work, but struggling to compromise helped me come to an important realization: marriage can bring incredible love into your life, but if you're not willing to make sacrifices for your partner, maybe marriage isn't right for you.

I loved Johnnie and I know he loved me, but he wanted a traditional wife and I wanted to be a comedian. I'm not willing to give up my dream to become someone's missus, no matter how fine he is. This might sound like a sad story to all those women who fantasize about finding Mr. Right. But for me, it had the happiest ending of all: if I hadn't given up my marriage I never would have become a worldwide touring comedian or been a CNN correspondent covering the inauguration of President Obama or written this book. Yes, I am single, but I am satisfied and loving my life.

# "We haven't set a wedding date, so why do you keep having bachelor parties?"

(Everything you need to know about nosy relatives, moody husbands, and the boyfriend who is taking forever to propose.)

*Dear Loni,*

*I've been living with my man for three years and everyone keeps asking when we're getting married. I like things the way they are. And besides, the idea of marriage makes me feel trapped. Do we really need to get married?*

*Signed,*
*Satisfied*

Dear Satisfied,

People get married for all kinds of reasons: some tie the knot because they're in love, others just love the tax write-offs.

I know one woman who got married because she wanted a lavish wedding. On her big day, Tish had eight ice sculptures, two dozen white doves, fourteen bridesmaids, six flower girls, and one drunken friend at the open-bar reception. (I had a great time.) Tish called me the very next day crying her eyes out saying she'd made a huge mistake. I told her *I* made a huge mistake with that last shot of Hennessy and needed a minute to get my head together before we had a serious talk. Three days later I called her back. She confessed that now that the fun of planning the wedding was over, she wasn't sure she wanted to be married.

These days Tish is happily single with a great wedding video and a hundred and twenty thousand dollars still owed to the caterer, band, and dove trainer. Don't make the same mistake Tish did. If the mere idea of walking down the aisle makes you feel "trapped," you definitely shouldn't be headed for the altar, no matter what anyone else says.

When I announced in 2002 that I was going to quit my engineering job to become a comedian, folks said I was crazy and I wasn't even that funny. I told my mother if I wanted her opinion I would ask for it. A year later, Momma Love sat with all her friends watching my first appearance on *The Tonight Show*. In other words: it's your life; do what makes *you* happy!

# "Oh, I *am* married.
# I just didn't invite you to the wedding."

## LONI LOVE'S BEST COMEBACKS FOR "WHY AREN'T YOU MARRIED YET?"

- "I like having sex with different men."
- "My ring finger looks better naked."
- "I like checking the 'single' box on my tax returns."
- "I don't need the two-for-one discount."
- "I don't want to share the remote."
- "I like sleeping in a queen-size bed alone with the Sunday paper, a bowl of popcorn, and some back issues of *Single and Satisfied Quarterly*."
- "I'm too much woman for just one man."

*Dear Loni,*

*I've been married seven years to a great guy. The other day I was at a jewelry store with my girlfriend and just for fun I decided to have my engagement ring appraised. I was shocked to find that all these years I've been wearing a fake diamond. My girlfriend says this is a "huge betrayal." What do you think?*

*Signed,*
*Did I Marry a Fraud?*

Dear Fraud,

Your friend is blowing things out of proportion. In my book, a "huge betrayal" is when a guy lies to you about what he can do in the sack.

Before you accuse your husband of false advertising, I suggest you give him the benefit of the doubt. Maybe your man thought the diamond *was* real. It's an honest mistake that anyone can make when they buy an engagement ring in the middle of the night, out of the back of a truck, from someone like my cousin Skillet. Or maybe he was broke and a cubic zirconia was all he could afford. Or maybe he wasn't sure the marriage would last. The bottom line is, I'm sure there is a perfectly good explanation.

Tell your husband you had the ring appraised and ask him what's up. I bet the two of you have a good laugh about it. And if it really bothers you to know you're rocking a fake rock, ask your husband for a real diamond for your next anniversary, birthday, or Kwanzaa gift. Or treat yourself to something sparkly you picked out and paid for yourself. You deserve it.

*Dear Loni,*

*I've been married six years and my husband has suddenly shut down. He barely talks to me anymore and has even stopped wearing his wedding ring. He says it's been giving him a rash, but I don't see any rash. What should I do?*

*Signed,*
*Put a Ring on It*

Dear On It,

If your husband is suddenly giving you the silent treatment and has taken off his ring, something has changed and you need to find out what it is. The problem is, men aren't always the best communicators. They feel perfectly fine staring at the TV for hours instead of opening up and saying what they really feel. Trust me on this; I know from experience.

One time I invited my Uncle Clifton to see one of my shows. The next day he told me he wanted to go shopping.

As we walked around the store, Uncle Clifton kept pulling dresses off the rack. Each was an elaborate floor-length gown covered in sequins, black lace, ostrich feathers, or all three. Finally I said to Uncle Clifton, "Look, if you're a cross-dresser, it's okay with me. But you really need to tell your wife." Uncle Clifton flew into a rage. The next thing I knew, sequins were flying through the air, feathers were everywhere, and both of us got kicked out of the store.

Later that night, when we had both calmed down, Uncle Clifton told me the dresses weren't for him. He wanted me to get one for myself because he thought I looked too casual when I did my act. He said, "You're my niece; you should hit the stage like Diana Ross!" I thanked him for his concern and explained that it just wasn't practical for me to do a show in Omaha, in August, wearing an evening gown and gloves. "I'm telling jokes," I told him. "Not singing 'Endless Love.'" My point is, it took Clifton getting kicked out of Big Mae's Dress Emporium and Beauty Supply before he could tell me what was on his mind.

If you want to know what's up with *your* man, don't expect him to volunteer the information. Instead, arrange to spend some time one-on-one, in a low-stress environment, so the two of you can really talk about how you feel about the relationship, your future together, and what makes you happy. Try inviting your husband for a long drive, a weekend at a bed-and-breakfast, or an impromptu Caribbean getaway. That way, if things don't work out, at least you'll come back with a tan.

# "No, you may not bring the flat-screen TV on our romantic weekend."

## LONI LOVE'S TOP FIVE GETAWAYS TO REKINDLE THE FLAME

- Go to a wine tasting so the two of you can reconnect and get tipsy at the same time.
- Take a cruise and get close while saving money by booking yourselves into the smallest cabin.
- See an out-of-town concert and buy tickets for the nosebleed seats so you can make out like teenagers.
- Take a drive to the country. Pull over and have sex on the side of the road. (Just make sure you drop off the hitchhiker you picked up before you get started.)
- Go to a Renaissance fair and tell him you're his wench for the weekend.

*Dear Loni,*

*My boyfriend and I have been together three years and have talked about getting married one day, but I'm still waiting for him to propose. Is it okay if I ask him to marry me? I already know exactly how I am going to do it!*

> *Signed,*
> *Let's Do This Already*

Dear Already,

Kudos to you for being a go-getter! Your eagerness to take the initiative must make you a firecracker at the office, and I bet you were at the top of your class at school. But in this situation, you may want to slow your roll.

My friend Eva wore the pants in her relationship with Louie. In fact, she not only wore the pants, she was a seamstress and would sew them herself. Eva would ask Louie out, choose the restaurant, make the reservations, and arrive at Louie's doorstep with his outfit for the evening and a list of approved discussion topics. How do you think this relationship worked out? That's right, it didn't. Louie went on to find a woman who let him pick out his own outfits, at least some of the time.

As much as some men behave like children, they still need to feel as though they are the ones in charge. And when it comes to marriage, most men like to be the one to propose.

For all you know, your man is taking his time because he's planning something really special, like a hot-air balloon ride, or teaching his pet parrot to say, "Marry me." Imagine how disappointed he would be if you beat his parrot to the punch.

Instead of proposing, why don't you spend your energy thinking of subtle ways to tell your man you're ready for him to pop the question? For instance, try making him dinner wearing a white dress and veil, replacing the porn site on his computer with YouTube wedding videos, or having your mom ask him when the two of you are going to stop breaking her heart and get married already.

> "One minute we're watching *Jerry Maguire,* the next minute he's asking me to marry him."

## LONI LOVE'S GUIDE TO WHEN HE'S MOST LIKELY TO PROPOSE

- After you dump him for the fiftieth time (but this time you *really* mean it!)
- While having sex in the closet during his aunt's Thanksgiving dinner
- After his dog has a near-death experience
- After mistakenly watching *Terms of Endearment*
- After he crashes your mom's car
- After the Las Vegas casino drops the charges
- After a wild weekend with the boys that he refuses to go into detail about
- When he realizes none of his frat brothers want to hang out and play beer pong anymore because they've all grown up

*Dear Loni,*

*My fiancé and I are getting married in six months and so far he's refused to help me plan the wedding. Does this mean he's getting cold feet?*

*Signed,*
*Worried*

Dear Worried,

Sweetie, I am a firm believer that when a man wants you to know something, he might not be able to articulate it, but he will send you a sign. On the flip side, sometimes women see signs where none exist. Maybe the fact that your man's not joining in the wedding planning has nothing to do with cold feet. Maybe he just doesn't want to pick out table centerpieces and bridesmaids' bouquets. And if your man *is* into matching the flowers to the table settings, well, you may have an entirely different problem on your hands.

If you really want to know if your man is having second thoughts, ask him to help you with something he might actually want to do and see how he responds. When my friend Liberty got married she asked her fiancé, Greg, to help with the flowers. Greg was usually very organized and dependable. But when it came to ordering the flowers, he kept missing the appointment with the florist. Liberty finally asked him what the deal was and he confessed he was worried he would mess things up and he didn't want her to be disappointed on her big day. That's when I understood why Liberty was so in love. Liberty decided to ask Greg to do something less stressful. She sent him to choose her lingerie for the honeymoon. She knew if he didn't get the right size it wouldn't matter. Those panties weren't going to stay on anyway.

You need to take a page from Liberty's playbook. If your man is into food, put him in charge of the dinner menu. If he's into music, have him pick the DJ. If he's a people person, put him in charge of keeping your two cousins who don't know they dated the same guy away from each other on the dance floor.

> ## "I should've known he didn't want to get married when he told me he was moving to the South Pole, alone."

### LONI LOVE'S SIGNS OF TROUBLE IN PARADISE

- He still hasn't signed the divorce papers his ex-wife sent over two years ago.
- He says he wants to keep his apartment as a "backup."
- The wedding is a week away and he still hasn't picked a best man.
- He keeps leafing through a Victoria's Secret catalog muttering, "Now I'm never going to live the dream."
- You still don't have a wedding date, but every Friday he has a bachelor party.
- You come home from work and the PlayStation console and his *Grand Theft Auto* and *Final Fantasy* video games are gone, but your *Dance Dance Revolution* is right where you left it.

*Dear Loni,*

*I am a professional woman with a great career. My fiancé is a struggling artist. I don't mind being the breadwinner in the family. But before we get married, I want him to sign a prenup agreement. How can I ask without insulting him?*

*Signed,*
*Protecting My Assets*

Dear Assets,

Men can be very touchy about money, especially if they don't have any. And if he's a painter he probably won't make money until he's dead.

The most important thing is to be sensitive to your man's feelings. Tell him, "I love you and I'm not going anywhere, but a prenup would give me peace of mind." If he refuses to sign, back off and give him some time before you bring it up again. If the two of you end up in a standoff with no one budging, you should figure out what's going on. Many couples get into arguments over money. But take it from me, when a man doesn't respect your desire to protect the money you worked hard for, it's usually a sign of more trouble to come. You may need to hash out your money issues with a professional counselor before you tie the knot.

And if all this fails, you can do what I always do when I

need someone to sign some papers against their will: I ask Skillet to sit them down for a friendly conversation until they change their minds.

*Dear Loni,*

*I thought I would be married by now, but I'm not. I feel like a failure. How can I stop feeling so bad?*

> *Signed,*
> *Life Didn't Turn Out the Way I Planned*

Dear Planned,

For most of us, life doesn't turn out the way we envisioned it when we were young. When I was a child, I wanted to be a singer. Unfortunately, I couldn't hold a B flat if you put it in my hand. But instead of clinging to an impossible dream, I evaluated my options and realized I can be happy, even if I can't sing like Beyoncé. (The voice is all she's got on me, though. When I put on my heels, a bodysuit, and a blond weave and dance around my bedroom to "Single Ladies," it's like we're practically twins.) Feeling satisfied with your life is something *you* control. You are the master of your destiny!

The queen of your queendom! Sometimes all you need to turn things around is a change of perspective. Instead of focusing on what you don't have, focus on what you do. Girl, what you need is a feel-good list.

Get a piece of paper and fold it into four quarters. In the top left quarter, write down all the wonderful things you have in your life, such as a warm bed, a full fridge, or a collector's edition of *The Bridges of Madison County* on Blu-ray. In the next quarter write a list of all the things you've accomplished, like graduating from college, building a wonderful career, or talking your way out of five speeding tickets. In the third quarter, list all the people who love you. Feel free to include the old man at the dry cleaner or the homeless guy who asked you to marry him last week. For your last list, write down all the people who bring a smile to your face. Definitely include pets and celebrities. Dr. Drew, my mom, and Mr. Chang, the owner of the Red Light liquor store, are all on my feel-good list.

Now take that piece of paper, fold it up, and stick it in your bra, next to your heart, where you can look at it any time you feel blue. That's where I keep my feel-good list, right beside my cell phone, my car keys, and a condom, just in case I get lucky.

*Dear Loni,*

*My boyfriend has been talking about marriage. I think I'm ready, but how do I know for sure?*

> *Signed,*
> *Undecided*

Dear Undecided,

It's good that you're giving this a lot of thought. Marriage can be a wonderful thing, but only if you're ready. If not, the situation can turn ugly fast. Not only do you have to get out of the marriage and potentially break your man's heart—you also have to return all the Crock-Pots and serving dishes you received as gifts. That's a lot of stamps.

My friend Maxine wasn't sure she was ready for marriage, but at thirty-five she felt time was running out, so when her boyfriend Jackson proposed, she said yes. For weeks leading up to the wedding, Maxine, a high school English teacher, kept trying to convince herself that she could get over Jackson's stinky breath, his poor performance in bed, and the fact that he said "ax" instead of "ask." Finally, the big day arrived. As Maxine and Jackson stood at the altar reciting their vows, Jackson looked at Maxine lovingly and said, "Baby, I knew the moment I axed you to marry me that we would live happily ever after." Maxine looked at Jackson and said,

"Baby, I love you too, but the word is 'asked.'" And with that, she ran out of the church.

Figuring out if you are ready for marriage requires some soul-searching. You have to ask yourself the Big Questions, like, am I willing to put someone's needs ahead of my own (at least occasionally)? Am I willing to compromise? Am I willing to accept mispronunciations, bad directions, and someone farting in my bed? Careful consideration can save you a lifetime of regret and a lot of postage returning all those gifts.

# "When you say 'till death do us part,' how long are we talking, exactly?"

## LONI LOVE'S "AM I READY FOR MARRIAGE?" QUESTIONNAIRE

- Are you familiar with, and willing to accept, any and all possible sounds that may be emitted by your future husband's body?
- Are you capable of losing an argument with dignity and grace? (And that means no throwing wine bottles against the wall.)
- Are you willing to help your husband feel needed, even if it means acting like you can't change a tire when you were the one who aced high school auto mechanics class?
- Do you possess the self-control to hold your smart-mouthed comments when your future hubby is acting like an idiot in front of his friends?
- Can you stay faithful to your husband after he's gained fifty pounds, stopped shaving, and decided he's most comfortable eating breakfast in the nude?
- Are you able to accept your husband's spending exorbitant amounts of money on items like a life-size personal robot when you are trying to save for something important, like an in-home nail salon?
- Do you own a personal vibrator?

If you've answered yes to most of these questions, congratulations, here comes the bride!

*Dear Loni,*

*I am a thirty-five-year-old professional woman with a great job, a nice condo, and a good relationship with my family. The only thing missing is a husband. I really want to get married in the next two years. How can I make my dream come true?*

*Signed,*
*Wife in Search of a Husband*

Dear Wife,

Only in the movies does a woman end up falling for her male best friend, or the stranger who pushes her out of the path of an oncoming truck, or the millionaire who hires her as a high-priced hooker. In the real world, meeting Mr. Right takes planning.

## Step One: Make a List

You know how I love a list! This list is all about the qualities you're looking for in a husband. For instance, your list might include "wants to have children," or "is religious," or "has a driver's license." Ha! I put that last one in to trick you. Having a driver's license shouldn't be on your list. Girl, you can teach him to drive! Your list should be things that you need for a happily-ever-after relationship. You're looking for Mr. Right, not Mr. Right Now.

Here's something on my list: Must be able to cook, clean the house, and do my taxes. As you can see, my Mr. Right list doubles as a job posting for a personal assistant.

## Step Two: Find Mr. Available

Remember back in the day when you would go out with someone just because he was cute and funny? Well, those days are over. You're on a mission and you should only be dating serious targets—er, I mean . . . prospects. Get the word out that you're looking to be fixed up on blind dates. Don't be shy. You're looking for the love of your life, so you need to act like a town crier. Tell your family, coworkers, hairdresser, postman, pastor, rabbi, shaman, married friends, and gynecologist. Let folks know you are open to any and all candidates, as long as the man is available for a serious relationship. That means no confirmed bachelors, nobody in the midst of a messy divorce, and no cousins.

## Step Three: Audition and Approve

Once you've started dating a prospective partner, you need to verify that he's husband material. Your audition process can involve many things. For instance, you might introduce him to a married friend to get her perspective. Or, if you want children, you might take him to your three-year-old nephew's birthday party to see how he gets along with kids. My friend Joleen was concerned that her boyfriend Nicholas wasn't able to hold up his end of the conversation. (By that she meant she didn't know if Nicholas had the stamina to listen to her mind-numbingly boring stories about what happened to her at work each day.) So one winter afternoon she suggested they go for a drive. She warmed up the car, had Nicholas wrap himself in blankets, gave him a warm cup of cocoa, and started to tell him about her week at the office. Any normal person would have been asleep before she pulled out of the driveway, but Nicholas is a trouper. He lasted for a good hour before his eyelids started to droop. That was long enough for Joleen to tell him about Monday's fiasco with the color copier and Thursday's coffeemaker scandal. Joleen gave her boyfriend an A-plus, and to this day they are still together.

## Step Four: Commit

If he's passed your audition, you can move on to the commitment phase, in which you both agree to date each other exclusively. Make sure he makes it official, with the appropriate Facebook status updates and Twitter posts, hashtag #I'mTaken!

## Step Five: Give Him a Timetable

Some women like you have a two-year plan. But whatever your timeline, once you've been in a monogamous relationship for a while, you have to take the initiative to move your relationship to the next phase. Tell your man you'd like to get engaged and married within the next year (or whatever timetable works for you). If he doesn't jump at the chance to lock you down, cut him loose and move on. Now, this is where a lot of women choke. A woman will tell her man she wants to get married and he'll say he needs "more time," or he's "not ready," or he loves you but "Momma isn't on board yet." That may be fine for the woman who is willing to be engaged for a decade. But that's not you.

## Step Six: Have a Life

One of the most important things for a woman to do while she searches for her soul mate is to focus on herself. Take some time, each and every day, to do something that has nothing to do with becoming a couple. Sign up for a yoga class, learn a new language, plan a girls' wild weekend. Sweetie, I support you in your quest to find a mate, but if I didn't remind you to love yourself first, I wouldn't be giving you the best advice I have.

# 9

# MESSY MESSY MESSES

$\mathcal{L}$*isten up, all my* drama queens: Are you always dating the wrong man? Are you constantly getting evicted from your apartment or kicked out of restaurants for throwing drinks at your frenemies? Are you not 100 percent sure who fathered your two youngest children? If you've answered yes to any of these questions, I hate to be the one to break it to you, but you're living a messy life. If that's the case, you owe it to yourself—and your family, friends, and coworkers—to consider the many benefits of cleaning up your act.

**Benefit number one: No more lying!**
Face it: if you live a messy life, you've probably had to tell a lot of lies. Chances are at some point you've had to explain how it is you ended up in the produce aisle of the grocery store with no pants on, or why you and your sister's ex-husband were passed out naked in your back-yard. And most of the time it's easier to make up a reason than tell the

truth about the bet you lost, the bender you went on, or the stupid idea that sounded great when your ex-convict boyfriend brought it up during a conjugal visit. But this just creates a tangle of lies, the details of which are often impossible to remember. When you live a mess-free life, you don't have to keep track of your lies by writing them in a notebook. You can just tell the truth. And if you can't remember the truth, well, honey, then you have a different kind of problem.

**Benefit number two: You don't have to hide the details of your love life from your closest friends.**
If you're the kind of woman who watches the nightly news and thinks to herself, *Oh, he's handsome!* when they cut to a scruffy guy in hand-cuffs being led away by police, you probably have poor judgment when it comes to men. And if your judgment is that poor, you've probably been in a series of relationships with sketchy guys, such as the time you found yourself in a whirlwind romance with a Colombian drug lord. The problem with these men is you can never tell your friends about them. And if you don't discuss your crazy relationships with your best friends, then there's no one around to tell you, "Girl, you've lost your damn mind!" Break the cycle now. If you're dating a man you feel you need to keep a secret, dump the guy and find someone you can take home to Mom.

**Benefit number three: You don't have to sneak around.**
Have you ever found yourself donning a wig and dark glasses to shop in a store with a clearly displayed poster that says you're not welcome? Do you feel it necessary to switch cars with your cousin every morning on your way to work "just as a precaution"? Have you ever had the need to print your own passport? C'mon now! That's no way to live. Constantly worrying that you're going to get caught in the

wrong place at the wrong time doing the wrong thing is very stressful. If you live a mess-free life, you can go anywhere and do anything with your head held high up and without wearing a disguise.

**Benefit number four: You get to make a whole new group of friends.**
If you want to rid your life of mess, you need to surround yourself with people who are living the life you aspire to lead. Make friends with stable, smart women who aren't out there dodging law enforcement or loan sharks. You can find women like this running animal shelters, volunteering on the PTA, or working as librarians. Do not look for them at your regular hangouts, loitering behind yellow police tape or passed out on the floor of the men's room after closing time. Notice how your new friends don't scream at each other in public or have the names of their baby daddies tattooed on their upper thighs. Their lives are calm and mess-free, and soon yours will be too.

**Benefit number five: Joy and happiness.**
The best part about cleaning up your messy life is that it will make you happy. You won't be worried about what other people think of you or be haunted by regret over things you should have done differently. And you won't have to pay to get that tattoo removed. Instead you'll be able to live in the moment, happy and satisfied and in love with yourself, which is exactly what you deserve.

# "My mother and stepfather divorced. Is it okay to date him?"

(Everything you need to know about dating your relatives, kids with big mouths, and the boyfriend who's got more lingerie in his closet than Victoria's Secret.)

*Dear Loni,*

*I've been happily married for three years and now we're expecting a baby. I'm worried because about six months ago I had a one-night stand while on a Caribbean getaway with my girlfriends. There was a lot of alcohol involved and I don't remember everything that happened. All I know is, I woke up naked with the gorgeous pool boy in my bed. Now there is a possibility that this baby I am carrying is not my husband's. What should I do?*

*PS: My husband is white and Malik totally is not.*

*Signed,*
*Regretting the Swirl*

Dear Swirl,

Sounds like your husband may be in for the shock of his life . . . or maybe not. The fact is, you don't know for sure that your husband isn't the father of your child, so there is no reason to make yourself sick with worry. In fact, you might be obsessing simply *because* you are pregnant. Pregnant women worry about everything. It's the hormones.

When my friend Simone was preggo, she was a ball of nerves. She fretted that she was gaining too much weight one day and not enough the next. She worried that the baby was kicking too much, then not enough. Mostly she just worried that the baby would come out looking like her husband's mother. (In fairness to Simone, I've seen her mother-in-law. I'd be scared too.)

But stress is bad for the baby and worrying is no way to get through a pregnancy. You need to get this off your chest. Here's what to do: write your husband a loving letter telling him how much you adore him, that you made a terrible mistake, and that you hope he'll be able to forgive you. And then explain that the baby might not be his. When you're finished, put the letter in a safety-deposit box at a bank you never go to, possibly in a different state. Then put this whole thing out of your mind. You've poured all your guilt and anxiety into your letter; now you must move on: set up the nursery and plan for the birth.

When that baby arrives, the whole family is going to be

full of excitement. Enjoy those days while you quietly inspect your child for signs of color. Check the ears. Momma Love always told me, the ears are the first place a baby gets color. If it's a boy, check the penis. Does the baby's penis look related to your husband, or is it more "Malik size," if you know what I mean?

If your husband is the dad, destroy the letter immediately. If not, get the letter and leave it on the kitchen table for your husband to read. Your husband will be angry, so be prepared for him to call you a whore, or, more likely, a ho, now that he knows you're into black guys. Also make sure you set up a session with a marriage counselor; you're going to need some professional help cleaning up this mess.

And, honey, the next time your horny girlfriends suggest a fun-filled getaway, offer to drive them to the airport and then take your ass back home, where it belongs.

> ## "I thought this was a nude beach. Why are we the only ones without any clothes?"

## LONI LOVE'S TOP GIRLFRIEND-GETAWAY VACATION BLUNDERS

- Giving your real cell number to the guy you met on the beach who said he wants to "move to the America" and something about a green card
- Not packing any condoms to avoid being "tempted"
- Coming home pregnant with no recollection of how you got that way
- Accidentally sending a picture of yourself holding a giant margarita and wearing nothing but water floaties to your entire office with the caption "Wish you were here, bitches!"
- Being your best friend's wingwoman on a singles cruise and letting it slip that she has a husband and four kids at home
- Taking your mother-in-law on your girlfriend's annual Caribbean weekend so you can "bond"
- Telling your boyfriend you are going away on business and having your BFF post pictures of you having the time of your life at Chippendale's Las Vegas on her Facebook page

*Dear Loni,*

*I've moved back home with my recently divorced mother after losing my job. Everything was fine until I came home late last night and heard some noise coming from my mother's room. It sounded like she was having sex! I'm so disgusted. What should I do?*

*Signed,*
*Totally Traumatized*

Dear Traumatized,

I understand times are tough, but nobody wants to hear their mom sounding like she's auditioning for a role in a Lil Wayne video. I remember the time I heard Momma Love getting it on. I was about twelve, and I came home from school early and the apartment was filled with the sound of squeaking bedsprings and a man's voice singing the Temptations' "My Girl." I haven't been able to listen to the Temptations without wanting to slap an old soul singer ever since. Girl, you need to double your hustle to get a job so you can move out of your mother's place ASAP.

In the meantime, give your mom some space. For instance, plan a once-a-week sleepover at a girlfriend's house and tell your mom well in advance so she can schedule her freak night. If you can't be out of the house for the whole evening, at least let your mother know what time you'll be coming home so she can plan her loudest activities for when you're gone.

The good news in this scenario is that your mother sounds like she's having a ball, or should I say *balls*. I'm guessing you're cramping her style as much as her new zest for life is making you blush. Move out and let Momma have her fun.

*Dear Loni,*

*My ex just got a job where I work. I still have feelings for him, but I know he has moved on and is dating someone else. I feel so bad when I see him. What should I do?*

*Signed,*
*No Options*

Dear Options,

Girl, I know just how you feel. There are times when I've had to do shows with male comics I used to date, but I've never refused a gig because of an old flame. One of my Rules of Love is "Money before honey." If it's a dude I really liked, I just put it in my act. That way I can talk about him and get paid at the same time.

You want to know the best way to take your mind off your ex? Look for a new job. In fact, your boyfriend coming to work at your company might be just the incentive you need to kick your career into high gear. I think you know what I'm going to tell you to do: make a list!

This list is your exit-strategy list, and it's going to include everything you need to make a successful exit from your job (and by that I mean leaving for something bigger and better). Your list should have at least fifty items on it. Some of the items might be simple, like "Revise résumé" or "Watch *Waiting to Exhale* for motivation." Other items might be more complicated, like "Take a road trip to another city where there are job opportunities and see if I'd like to live there." Maybe you need to take a class or get some special training. Sign up! But don't stop there: update your interview wardrobe, buy some new work shoes, or treat yourself to a weave.

Slowly work your way through your exit-strategy list. It should take you at least six months. And guess what happens then? Either you'll have landed a new job, or you'll be over your ex (but with classy new hair extensions and the confidence to ask for a raise). Either way, you win.

> ### "I wouldn't have taken this job if I had known my ex-husband's new girlfriend was going to be my supervisor."

## LONI LOVE'S MESSIEST WORKPLACE SCENARIOS

- Conducting a team-building workshop with your ex's current wife and the woman he's cheating on her with
- Interviewing your ex for a server position at the Blimpie you're managing
- Breaking off your wedding engagement to your supervisor so you can date his hot new intern
- Finding your boss, with his pants down, sitting on the photocopier
- Having to fire your husband and hire someone half his age

*Dear Loni,*

*A few years ago my husband suggested we have an open relation-ship. At first I was totally against it, but I've come to love our ar-rangement. Seeing other people for the occasional fling keeps me feeling sexy! The problem is, my husband has grown very jealous of my escapades and wants us to become monogamous again. How can I get him to change his mind?*

*Signed,*
*In the Swing of Things*

Dear Swing,

It's pretty obvious that when your man proposed this idea, he thought *he* was the one who was going to be having all the fun. Now that he's discovered your hidden talent as a man juggler, he's not so happy. I'm not surprised. Men often come up with "great ideas" that are only great in their imaginations. One time Roscoe and I made a bet about which dude on *Maury* was really the baby's father. Whoever lost had to fulfill the other's secret fantasy. Well, I lost, and the next thing I knew I was accompanying Roscoe to a swingers party. As you probably know, a swingers party is a get-together at someone's home where horny consenting adults can do whatever, however, with whomever.

When we arrived, it was like a scene from *Caligula*. Naked

folks were everywhere: on the floor, in the bathroom, in the pantry, even in the oven. A beautiful woman was standing by a pool table holding a cue and wearing no pants. A middle-aged guy was under the pool table giving the woman what I call "the kiss of life." Roscoe was in heaven. I could see the excitement in his eyes . . . and by that I mean his pants. I went to the bar, poured myself a drink, and found a dry couch to sit down on. "Roscoe," I said, "this is what you wanted. Knock yourself out. You have until my glass of Hennessy is empty, and then I'm leaving." Two minutes later Roscoe came running back saying, "Let's get out of here!" In the car Roscoe told me that a big burly man had approached him and asked if he could toss his salad and "make a pie." "Loni," Roscoe said, "I don't know what the hell he meant by 'make a pie,' and I sure wasn't about to find out."

If you really want to keep up your end of this arrangement, you're going to have to remind your husband of why he wanted an open marriage in the first place. Try fixing him up on a date. If he has a great time, you're both in business. If, on the other hand, your husband still wants to call it quits, I suggest you rewatch your wedding video, put on some Barry White, break out the K-Y jelly, and get it on with the man you married.

# "His-and-hers Beer Koozies is not what I meant when I said I wanted something 'romantic' for my birthday."

## LONI LOVE'S IDEAS THAT NEVER WORK OUT THE WAY MEN THINK THEY WILL

- Barbecuing naked
- Taking two Viagra pills at once to "double the pleasure"
- Trying to get you in the mood by taking you to a Vegas topless revue, instead of the Céline Dion concert you wanted to see
- E-mailing porn videos of himself to your work e-mail
- Hitting the emergency stop button on the elevator so you two can have an impromptu make-out session
- Buying you sexy lingerie two sizes too small because he thinks you'll take it as a compliment

*Dear Loni,*

*My mother and my stepfather, Rick, divorced a few months ago. Rick is very handsome and only fifteen years older than me. We've always had great chemistry. In fact, we get along better than he and my mother ever did. Do you think it's okay for me to ask Rick out on a date?*

*Signed,*
*(Step) Daddy's Girl*

Dear Daddy's Girl,

I'm always surprised by how often I have to repeat this, but here it goes again: I don't care how fine, rich, or charming a man is, a woman should never date her mother's ex. Unless, of course, you're trying out for a spot on *The Jerry Springer Show*.

When I was starting to date, Momma Love would stress to me the importance of not mixing romance and relatives. Her favorite motto was, "The same DNA don't share P and A." I didn't learn until I was in college that the "P" was for "penis" and "A" stood for "ass." I thought it stood for "peanuts" and "apples," which is why I still don't like sharing food with my cousins.

Of course, not everybody follows this Rule of Love. A few years ago, my friend Rita started dating her sister's ex.

Rita claimed that Pauline gave her the okay, but Pauline's true feelings came out over Thanksgiving dinner at Rita's house. After the meal, the alcohol was flowing and everyone was getting loose. Suddenly, Pauline got up from the chair, grabbed her plate, marched around the table to where her sister was sitting, and dumped her turkey bones, corncobs, and uneaten broccoli onto Rita's lap. When Rita said, "What the hell are you doing?" Pauline shouted back, "Obviously, you love taking my leftovers. I thought I'd hand-deliver them this time!" Suddenly the two women were rolling on the floor locked in a sister-on-sister brawl.

The only way dating your stepfather can possibly turn out okay is if your mother has been secretly eyeing one of your exes and you offer her a one-to-one Man Trade. But of course, that's still going to land you on *Jerry Springer*.

*Dear Loni,*

*I've been dating this wonderful, kind, and caring man. Last week he confessed that he was "born into the wrong body." Meaning, he used to be a woman. He explained that he's had surgery and can do everything I would expect a man to do, except get me pregnant. I love being with my boyfriend, but I am so confused.*

*Signed,*
*I Love Him But . . .*

Dear But,

I don't blame you for being confused. I once dated a man named Terrell who turned out to be a member of the religious rap group Righteous Gangsters. Their big hit was a single called "Jesus Is an O.G." Two weeks into our relationship Terrell told me that the RGs fast every Friday. No eating on Fridays? Where I come from, Friday is date night. I eat on date night. As soon as I heard that, I knew that our relationship would never work out.

I think you should give yourself some time to let the news sink in. Don't give up on a relationship just because the person you're in love with has a few skeletons—or in this case, heels and panties—in his closet.

This is a great time for you to ask your boyfriend plenty of questions so you can really understand his situation. Then see how you feel. If you'd like to cool it on the romance while you figure things out, that's okay too. This man loves and cares about you; I wouldn't kick him out of your life just because he had his plumbing rerouted. Now, if he tells you he doesn't eat on Fridays, that's a whole different story.

*Dear Loni,*

*I'm a white woman dating a black man. We are very much in love and talking about getting married. The problem is my father is not so open-minded. When I took my boyfriend over for dinner, my father made an offensive racial remark and now my boyfriend says even if we get married he will never eat at my parents' house again. What should I do?*

*Signed,*
*Stuck in the Middle*

Dear Stuck,

America is filled with so many beautiful races and cultures. With all that mixing and mingling, some of us are bound to find love across the color lines. I know I did! Years ago, I dated a man named Wang. I'd never dated outside my race before, but Wang was a real cutie and sweet to boot. Our first date was at his family's restaurant; Wang set a beautiful table with candles and flowers. I was looking forward to our romantic dinner when Wang's father came from the kitchen, put a dish on the table, and announced, "I made chicken. Black people love chicken!"

He turned to head back to the kitchen, but I was right behind his ass, telling him I did not appreciate his comments. "Not all black people love chicken," I told him. "I happen to favor bacon." To his credit, Wang's father apologized profusely and brought us a plate of bacon instead. Before he took the chicken away, I snuck a taste. That chicken was delicious! I had him wrap me up some to go.

You need to let your father know that if he doesn't join the rest of us in the twenty-first century, he's going to risk losing his daughter and all those little soy-mocha-latte grandbabies you're going to be having. If your father has any sense, he'll man up and apologize to your boyfriend the way Wang's father apologized to me. If not, plan on going to your boyfriend's family for the holidays. Just don't bring a chicken.

*Dear Loni,*

*I was at an Usher concert when my boyfriend's very married best friend showed up with another woman on his arm. I want to tell his wife, who happens to be a good friend of mine. My boyfriend said if I "snitch" on his friend, he'll break up with me. What should I do?*

*Signed,*
*Divided Loyalties*

Dear Divided,

I understand your impulse to tell his wife. If I had information like this about a friend's husband, I would want to sing it from the mountaintop. But not before I smacked that man upside his head. Your boyfriend doesn't want you to tell because he thinks that would be breaking his Guy Code. But we women have to stick together. Not only was this creep creeping, this was an Usher concert! Shout-out to Usher! Ever since I pushed him into the bathroom at the *Chelsea Lately* show for a private conversation, Usher's been my second boo, right after Dr. Drew.

Girl, there is a simple way out of this mess. Find a mutual friend with a really big mouth, leak the information to her, and let her be the one to break it to your friend. Try your gossiping hairdresser, a chatty-Cathy neighbor, or the grocery store clerk who can't keep a secret. There is nothing better than getting gossip at the checkout stand. If you use coupons, you can save money at the same time.

> "The only way your man is a 'regional manager' is if he thinks the fryer station at McDonald's is a region."

## LONI LOVE'S GUIDE TO THINGS YOU SHOULD ALWAYS TELL YOUR FRIENDS ABOUT THEIR HUSBANDS

- You find a YouTube video of him wearing your friend's favorite dress and lip-synching "Single Ladies."
- You catch him outside an abortion clinic with his intern.
- You see him standing on the highway with a sign that reads, "Will do ANYTHING for money."
- You sit next to him on a long flight and he has eight beers before takeoff.
- You take your five-year-old to a Wiggles concert and he's there with no child.

*Dear Loni,*

*I'm a single mother. My boyfriend and I just broke up, but we've remained friends. A few weeks ago, when a new man picked me up to take me to dinner, my daughter wouldn't stop talking about my ex. Then, when my ex came over later that week for game night, my daughter kept talking about my "new boyfriend." Now my new man is mad, my ex is jealous, and I am furious at my daughter. What should I do?*

*Signed,*
*Living with a Security Leak*

Dear Security,

People tell single mothers they should be careful about dating too many men because it sets a bad example for the child. But your story proves that single moms need to be careful about dating because their child can mess up their game! You see, children are like broken tape recorders. They record everything, but when you hit "playback" all you get is a garbled mess. One time, my friends Mike and T.J. asked me to babysit their children so they could go out for a romantic dinner. Of course I said yes. Those children are like family to me, plus Mike and T.J. always keep a well-stocked bar.

After the children were soundly asleep, I poured myself a nightcap. I don't like to drink alone, so I invited over

Duran, my honey at the time. Duran and I started watching *Ghostbusters,* which was playing on TV. The classics always make me drowsy. The next thing I know, I'm sound asleep with Duran snoring like a freight train on top of me. He was hugging on me like I was a human pillow.

I don't know how long we were knocked out, but when I woke up, all three of the children were standing in front of us, dressed in their little footie pajamas. "We want apple juice," said Naomi. "And why are you sleeping with that man?" said her younger brother Byron. And "Ooooh, I'm telling," added the four-year-old Junior, aka "Little Bigmouth."

The next morning at breakfast (of course, I wasn't leaving without some of T.J.'s delicious bacon and eggs), Naomi started flowing like the river Jordan with her recap of the evening. "Auntie Loni was drunk!" she said. "And doing it on the sofa! And she was naked!" Then the other two started chiming in like Christmas bells. "Aunt Loni was having a party!" cried Byron. "And then," added Little Bigmouth, "she turned into a vampire!"

By the time breakfast was over, T.J. and Mike were signing me up for AA and a community-college course on being a good role model. The bottom line is, keep your daughter away from your dates. What she doesn't know, she can't talk about.

*Dear Loni,*

*I am having a very difficult time with my new relationship. I love my boyfriend very much, but he keeps expecting me to pay for everything. I make more money than he does, so I guess it makes sense. But still, it doesn't feel right. What do you think?*

*Signed,*
*Miss Moneybags*

Dear Moneybags,

I've been in this situation before, so I know just how you feel. When I was an engineer, I dated a struggling jazz musician named Charlie. He could play the trumpet like no other but he was broke as a joke, so I had to pay for everything. I paid for our dates, his sheet music—hell, I even "loaned" him money so he could give it to his mother to help pay her mortgage. I did this because I loved Charlie and we were in a serious relationship. He had talent and I wanted to see him succeed, but I began to feel like he was taking advantage of the situation. Especially after he took my credit card to order me flowers for my birthday. Imagine, he couldn't even scrape together fifty bucks to show his love on my special day!

Girl, remember this Rule of Love: no matter how little money he makes, if he isn't willing to spend some of his hard-earned cash on your birthday, he doesn't love you. Sure, he may like you, but it's definitely not love.

Finally, I gave Charlie an ultimatum: either he get a job and start pulling his own weight, or I was going to end our relationship and tell his mother the truth about where he got that money he'd been giving her. Well, guess how this story turned out? Charlie's mother paid me back my money and I used it to take a vacation with my new boyfriend.

Honey, you deserve to be treated like the beautiful woman you are. Treat yourself well, and expect no less from everyone in your life. And when it comes to men, always remember my first Rule of Love: you can love him or leave him, but don't get stuck with the tab.

# Acknowledgments

To begin, *I'd like* to thank the Academy! Oh, sorry. Wrong speech.

A year ago, this book was just a dream. Like most dreams, it took a team to turn it into a reality. Now here's the fun part where I get to give my thanks to everyone who helped me make my dream come true.

First of all, a shout-out to my manager, Judi Brown Marmel. Hey, Judi! Thank you for sticking with the fat chick all these years. You are the best manager a girl could have. Without your support and passion for this project, there would be no book. And now look. More than two hundred damn pages! I'll never forget how you flew to New York and helped me sell this idea to the good folks at Simon & Schuster. You are officially the best wingwoman ever! I love you, Judi!

Next up, Jeannine. Girl, what can I say? I couldn't have picked a more talented writer to work with. During those late-night bicoastal girl talks, I could always count on you to ask the right question, offer great insight, and help me make sense.

And a special shout-out to Jeannine's daughter, Niko, who would answer the phone and occasionally remember to tell her mom I called. Niko, honey, you aren't old enough to read this, so now that you've seen your name, step away from the book.

Special thanks to my editor extraordinaire, Sarah Knight. Thank you for your enthusiasm for this project and your most helpful feedback. Although I'm not sure why you kept asking for more jokes about anal sex. But I guess that's between you and your husband.

And Miss Brandi Bowles from Foundry Literary + Media, thank you for making this deal happen. You really *get* me and I appreciate that.

Dominic Friesen, my publicist, and his right-hand woman, Amy, who work tirelessly spreading the message of Love, thank you. Like Momma Love always told me, every girl needs a gay BFF.

To the Levity team, Robert, Melissa, Ray, Derek, and Erin, thank you for making me one of the top comics on the club circuit, encouraging me to do this book, and supporting me through the process.

To Hilary, Sheila, Tomii, and Stu at Telepics, thank you for believing in me and continuing to support my love of helping women.

And a very special thank-you goes to Les Moonves, president and CEO of CBS, who handpicked me in 2003 to appear on *Star Search.* You gave me my first opportunity to do stand-up in front of a national TV audience and jump-started my career. I will be forever thankful. Even though I didn't win. Les, you and I both know I was robbed!

To Steve, Ian, Barbara, and David at Innovative Artists, thank you for being so diligent about getting me work and listening to my dreams, and for always doing your best to help them come true.

And to that big ole lush Chelsea Handler: Girl, thank you for taking me along for the ride. You're a trailblazer who's inspired me every step of the way. It's been a real honor being the butt of your jokes. And a special thanks to the *Chelsea Lately* staff and crew for making me feel like part of the family.

Of course, my thank-yous wouldn't be complete without a special shout-out to Dr. Drew Pinsky and Susan Pinsky for being my Boo and Mrs. Boo.

On a personal note, a special thank-you goes to my girl Vanessa Graddick for her friendship, support, and encouragement, and for reading the manuscript and suggesting I go topless on the cover.

To Willis, DeSean, Jeff, and Ralph, thanks for being the best feature acts a girl could ask for.

And to my tried-and-true, ride-or-die, through-thick-and-thin—well, mostly thick—friends to the end, Rosa, Monique, Ken, Rod, Yvette, and Sherri, thank you for always being there when I need you.

To the ladies at *Café Mocha,* MC Lyte, Angelique, and Sheila, thank you for surrounding me with love and good talk every Monday.

And last but most certainly not least, the biggest thank-you of all goes out to my wonderful and amazing fans! Have I ever told you how much I love those sweet and encouraging messages you send? How I love seeing your faces light up when I'm onstage? How I miss you on my days off and wish you were there to go grocery shopping with me? I appreciate each and every one of you. It's a privilege to make you laugh.

This is Jeannine. I'd like to chime in here to say thanks to Loni. Thank you for choosing me to help you bring this book to life. Hearing you laugh (mostly at your own jokes) was the highlight of my week! You are funny and kind and an absolute joy to work with.

# About Loni Love

Comedian Loni Love was raised by a single mother in the famous Brewster-Douglass housing projects in Detroit, Michigan, childhood home to such notables as Diana Ross and Lily Tomlin. Life wasn't always easy. But as a child, Loni was a hard worker and a good student with an irrepressible desire to make folks laugh.

That impulse has served her well. These days Loni is one of the most beloved entertainers in America, with millions of fans who treat her as though she is their very best friend. Loni, who graduated from Prairie View A & M University with a degree in engineering, worked briefly as a project manager at Xerox before launching her comedy career. She quickly made a name for herself with her irreverent take on current affairs and her warm and engaging style. In 2003, Loni won national acclaim after making it to the finals on *Star Search* and being recognized by both Comedy Central and *Variety* magazine as one of the "top ten comics to watch." Since then, she has become a TV staple, appearing on VH1, E!, TruTV, CNN, and Disney, and holding court as one of the most hilarious panelists on E!'s hit show *Chelsea Lately*.

Loni, who also cohosts the nationally syndicated *Café Mocha* radio program, says that despite her success, her greatest thrill still comes from connecting with her fans at her live shows. "I don't believe in just being funny," she says. "I believe in making people feel good about themselves. That's why I do what I do. I want to spread the joy."

## Jeannine Amber

Jeannine Amber is a magazine writer who has won numerous professional awards for her investigative features but says, "Working with a comedian is much more fun."

She holds a master's degree from Columbia University's Graduate School of Journalism and lives and writes in Brooklyn, New York, with her daughter, Niko, and their dog, Bubbles. Read more of Jeannine's work at JeannineAmber.com.